ARCHI-
DOODLE

Dedicated to Henry, who was a wonderful man,
a brilliant dad and a great carpenter.

LAURENCE KING

Published in 2013
by Laurence King Publishing Ltd
361–373 City Road
London EC1V 1LR
Tel +44 20 7841 6900
Fax +44 20 7841 6910
E enquiries@laurenceking.com
www.laurenceking.com

Reprinted 2014, 2015, 2016

A catalogue record for this book is available from the British Library

ISBN 978 178067 321 9

Designed by Matt Cox for Newman and Eastwood
Cover design by Pentagram
Project editor: Gaynor Sermon
Printed in China

ARCHI-DOODLE

AN ARCHITECT'S ACTIVITY BOOK

STEVE BOWKETT

LAURENCE KING PUBLISHING

Various views of Clayton House,
Buckinghamshire, England.
Aldington Craig and Collinge, 1966

Introduction

This book is for anyone who is interested in architecture, particularly those of you who like to draw, doodle and dream about our built environment. It is organized around a series of design drawing exercises that range from the amusing to the academic, from the informative to the inspirational. The buildings and landscapes that I have selected to draw should act as a stimulant for creative new architectural designs while also illustrating some of the concepts that underpin 'modern' architecture.

While my drawings in this book are all monochrome, somewhat clean and executed using a fine-line pen (for the sake of clarity), you are encouraged to experiment with a variety of representational media in your renderings; pens, pencils, paint, charcoal, collage, and so on. It is also my intention that you use the illustrations in the book to experiment with colour, doodle around the edges and on top of the drawings, and of course draw in the bigger spaces provided.

This is not a book about *how* to draw buildings – there are plenty of those to choose from – but a book about *what* to draw, and it should be treated as a journal, sketchbook or even as a primer for putting your portfolio together. Having said that, I have given the first few pages over to some tips on basic tools and techniques to get you started.

I hope that this book will be useful and inspirational for architects, students, teachers, parents and their children, but – most importantly – that it will be fun to work with.

About the author

Steve Bowkett is passionate about good design. He has taught and practised architecture for over 25 years in numerous universities and colleges and is currently a senior lecturer at London South Bank University in the UK. He studied architecture at the Royal College of Art in London and the Polytechnic of Central London.

Steve and his partner Jane have three daughters, Zoe, Sadie and Phoebe, and live in Buckinghamshire, where Steve pursues a serendipitous life.

Equipment

These are the basic tools that you might consider using in this book.

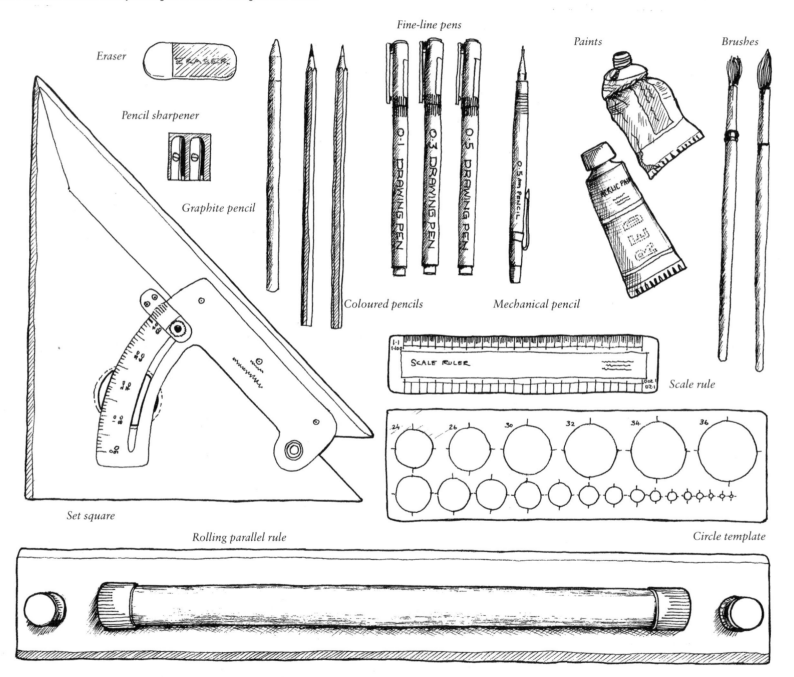

Eraser

Pencil sharpener

Graphite pencil

Fine-line pens

Coloured pencils

Mechanical pencil

Paints

Brushes

Set square

Scale rule

Rolling parallel rule

Circle template

Techniques

This page shows a selection of the techniques that I have used to create the drawings in this book. These simple skills will provide you with the means to build texture and form, add shadow and increase density, and create a range of different material effects.

Hatching

Cross hatching

Stippling techniques

Selection of material effects: coral; sediment; grasses; gravel; foliage; vegetation; rippled water; surface texture

Plans, Sections, Elevations, Axonometric

These two pages show the convention of how an architectural orthographic drawing is made of a building. The drawing on the far left is an axonometric drawing with a line showing where the cut is to be made to reveal the sectional drawing below it. The drawing under the section is the side view or elevation of this building.

On the opposite page the axonometric has been cut to reveal the interior rooms of the upper floor of the building. The two drawings below this are the corresponding roof plan and upper-floor plan.

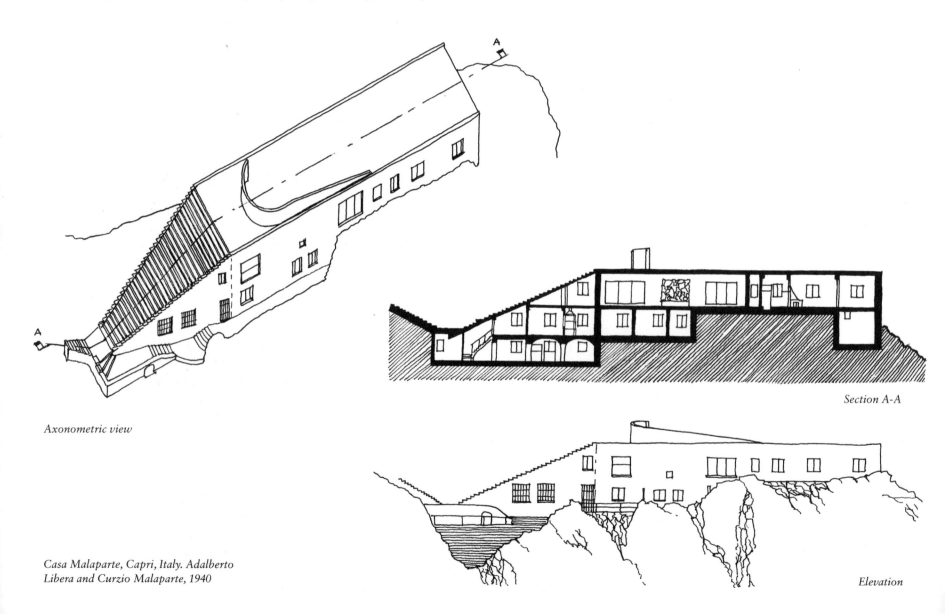

Section A-A

Axonometric view

Casa Malaparte, Capri, Italy. Adalberto Libera and Curzio Malaparte, 1940

Elevation

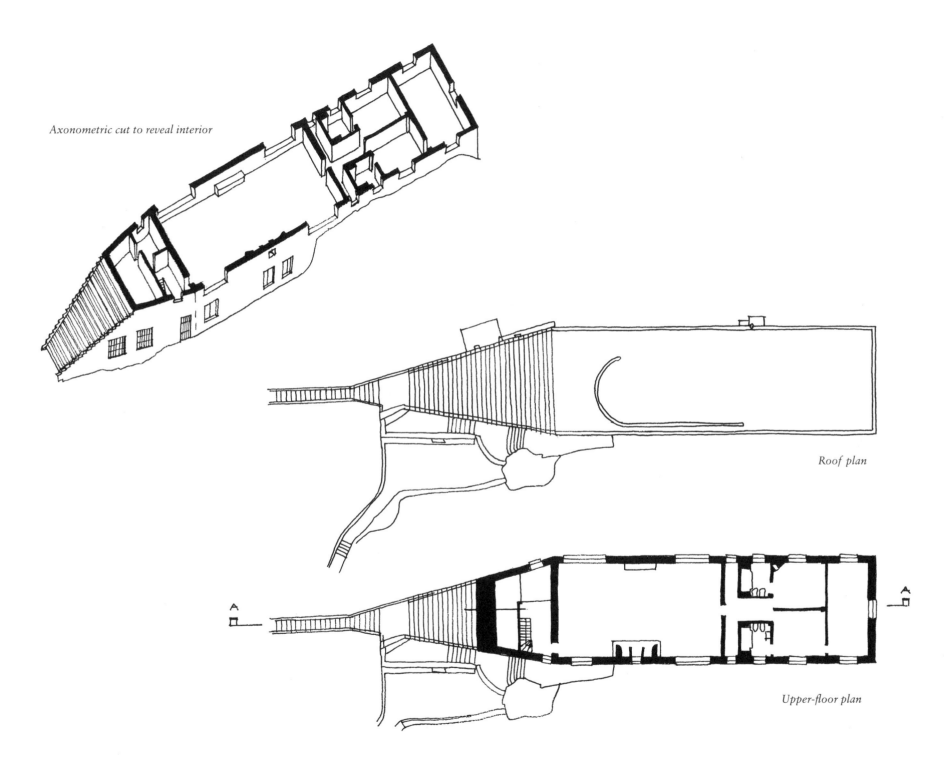

Axonometric cut to reveal interior

Roof plan

Upper-floor plan

These are currently the world's **tallest buildings**.

Draw your version of a skyscraper for the new millennium.
Give it a name… ➡➡

600m	
450m	
300m	
150m	

Burj Khalifa
Dubai, UAE
828m (2,717ft)

Freedom Tower
New York City, USA
541m (1,776ft)

Taipei 101
Taipei, Taiwan
508m (1,677ft)

World Finance Center
Shanghai, China
492m (1,614ft)

Petronas Towers
Kuala Lumpar, Malaysia
452m (1,483ft)

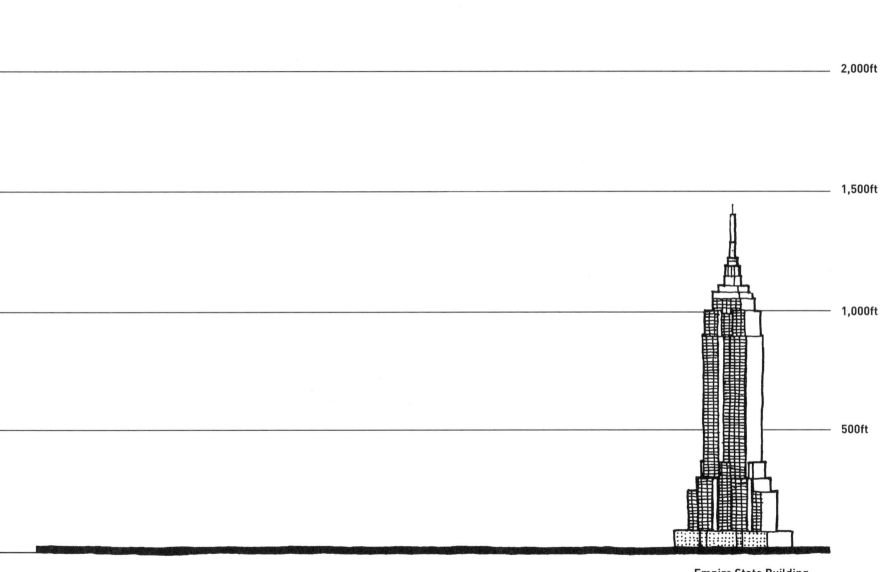

2,000ft

1,500ft

1,000ft

500ft

Empire State Building
New York City, USA
443m (1,453ft)

The Sony Tower has a **famous roof,** a 'Chippendale Tallboy'
classical pediment top. This iconic skyscraper needs a new image and a new top.
Look at other design objects such as furniture to influence the form.

*Add to some of these other iconic skyscrapers
with memorable rooftops...*

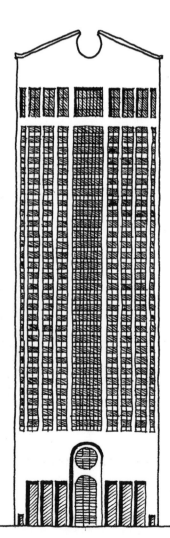

*AT&T Building, New York,
USA. Philip Johnson and John
Burgee, 1984*

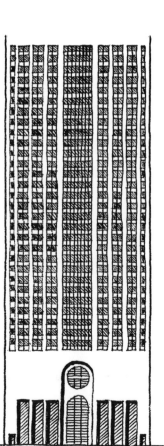

Al Hamra Tower, Kuwait City. S.O.M. 2011; Chrysler Building, NYC. William Van Alen, 1930; Empire State Building, NYC. Shreve, Lamb and Harmon, 1931; The Shard, London. Renzo Piano, 2012.

Complete the drawings of the following **famous buildings**.

The Taj Mahal, Agra, India.
Ustad Ahmad Lahauri, 1653

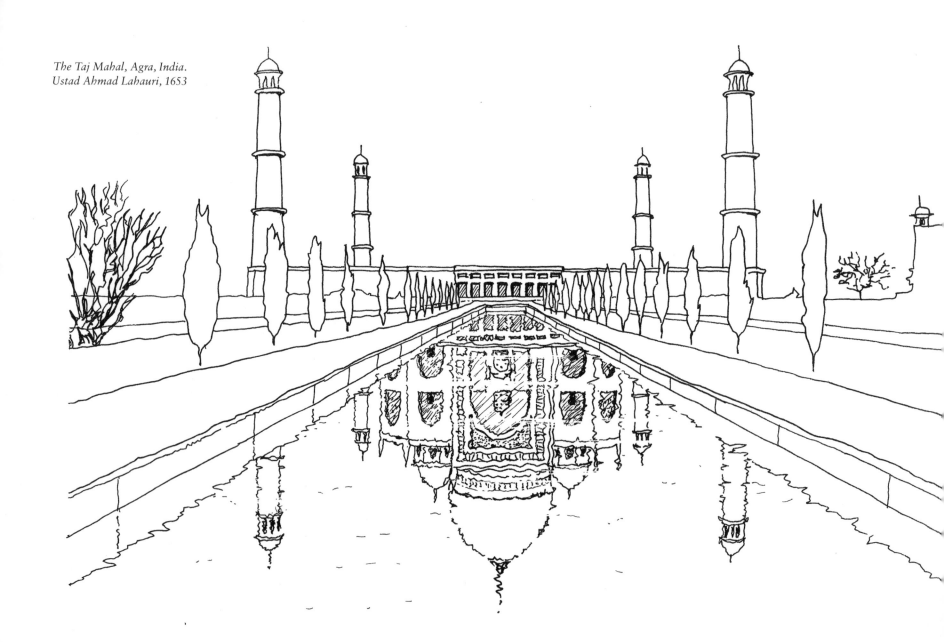

The Eiffel Tower, Paris, France.
Gustave Eiffel, 1889

Cities beneath our great oceans may well provide a new way of living in the future. The structure below was influenced by the shape of coral.

Design your own underwater community in the space provided... ➤➤

Here are a variety of different **bridge designs**.

Use their structural principles to help you design a new bridge to expand this town across the sea...

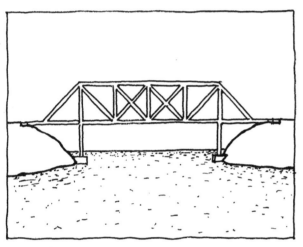

Truss bridge

Cantilever bridge

Suspension bridge

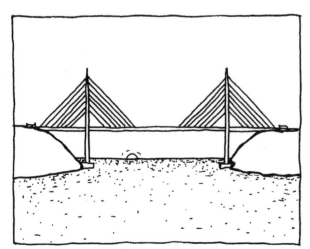

Cable-stayed bridge

Arch bridge

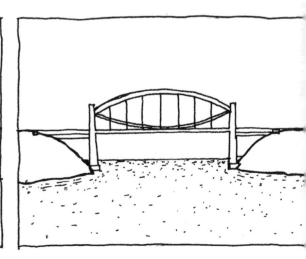

Lenticular-truss bridge

Create a bridge over a wide river...

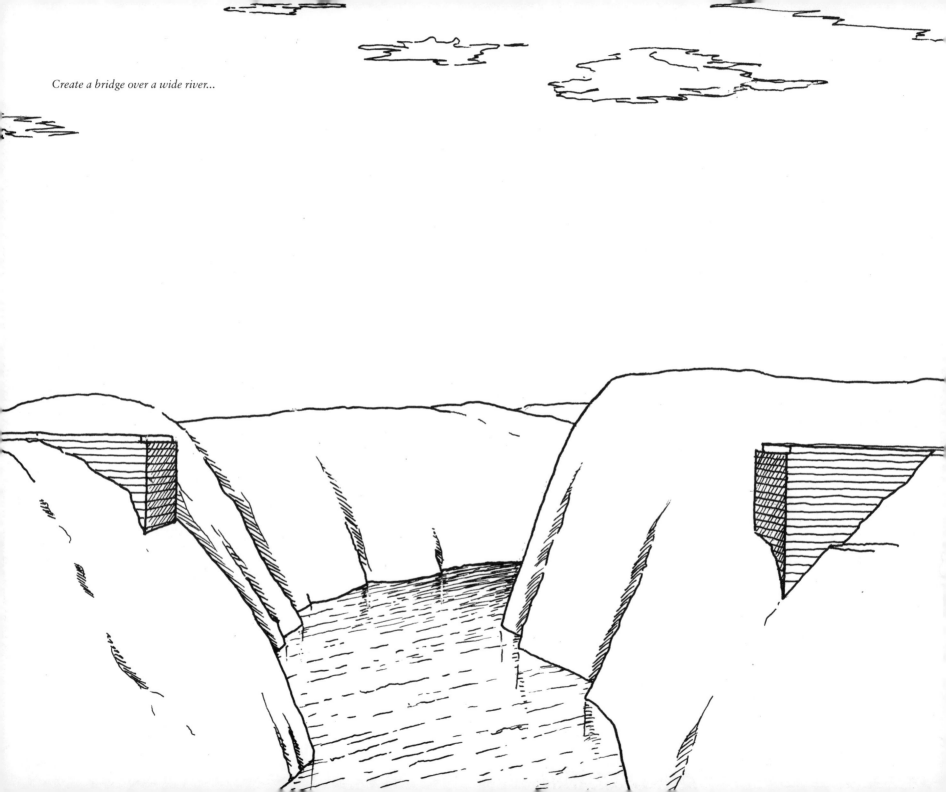

And over a highway...

In Dubai they have created a series of **new islands** along the coastline.

Design your own new island community... ▶▶

Palm Islands, man-made archipelago,
Dubai, UAE. Conceived by Sheikh
Mohammed bin Rashid Al Maktoum,
developed by Nakheel Properties, 2003-08

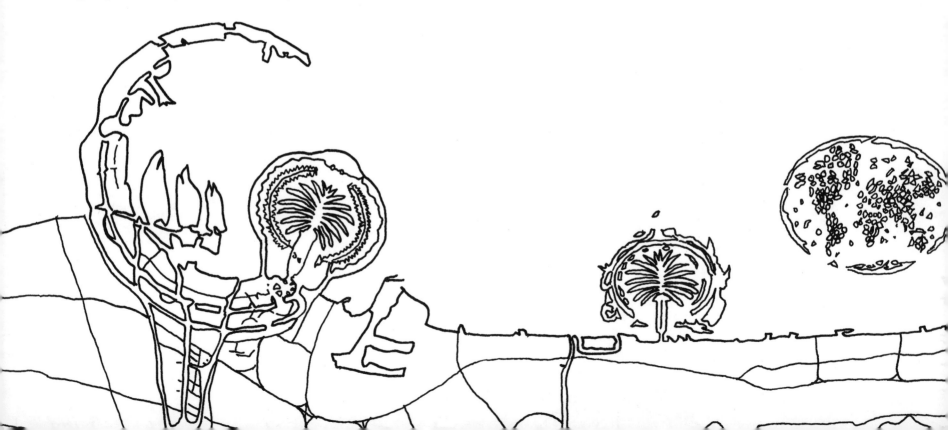

'The architect of the future will **build imitating Nature'**
— Antonio Gaudí

Design the external envelope of a building that resembles
something found in nature...

Casa Batlló, Barcelona, Spain.
Antonio Gaudí/Josep Maria Jujol, 1906

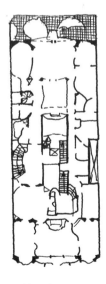

Plan drawing

Here are six examples of how the same room can be altered to **manipulate light** and space using different forms of window opening.

Use the same interior room proportion to draw your own ideas...

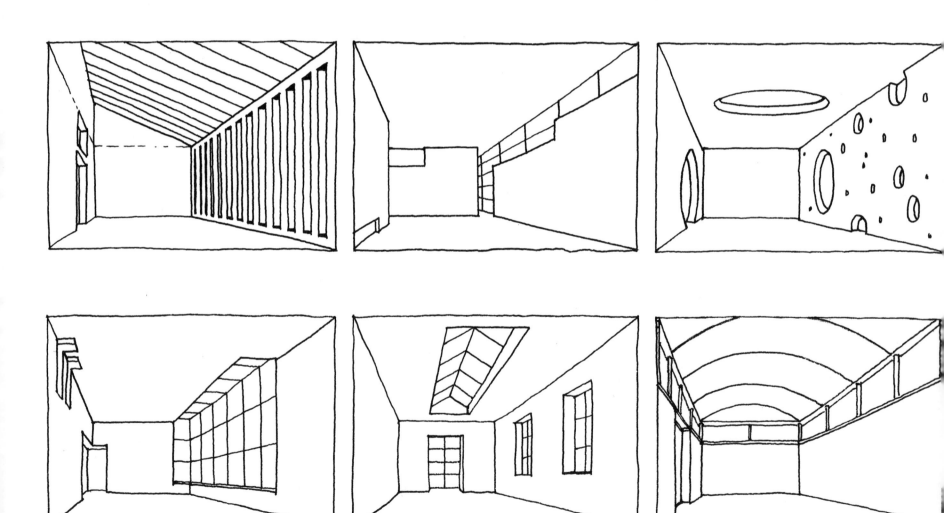

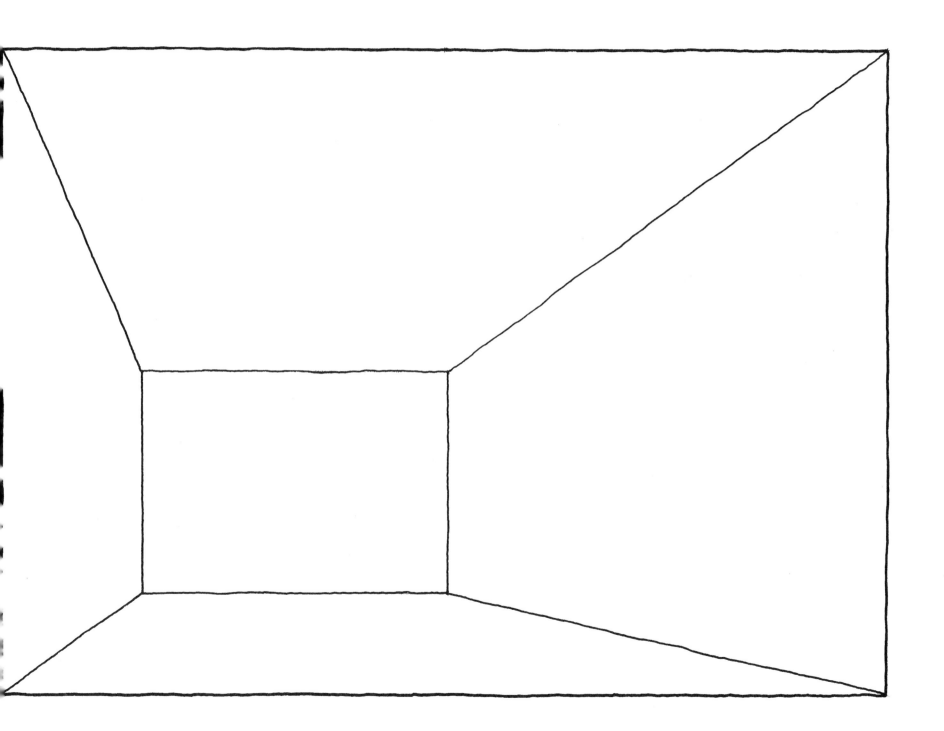

Theis and Khan designed a new **sacred space** while converting a
London church, using the concept of a beam of light pouring through the roof.

*Using the shell of the existing building, design and draw an idea
for a new space using light to generate the form...*

*Lumin United Reform Church, London, England.
Theis and Khan Architects, 2008*

*Section showing the walls of the 'light beam'
and the space within*

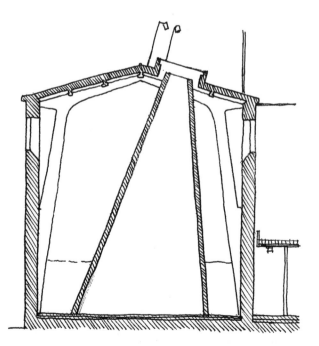

When designing the **roof of a building** here are a variety of forms to consider.

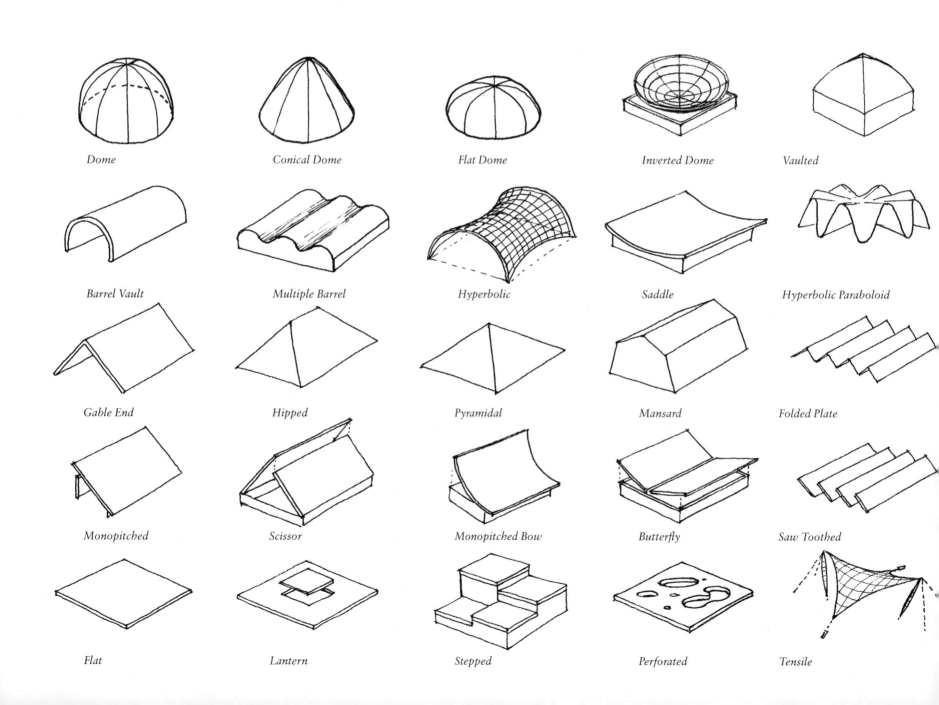

Dome	Conical Dome	Flat Dome	Inverted Dome	Vaulted
Barrel Vault	Multiple Barrel	Hyperbolic	Saddle	Hyperbolic Paraboloid
Gable End	Hipped	Pyramidal	Mansard	Folded Plate
Monopitched	Scissor	Monopitched Bow	Butterfly	Saw Toothed
Flat	Lantern	Stepped	Perforated	Tensile

an you come up with some other roof types? ➡

The **Sydney Opera House** is dominated by its shell-like roof structure sitting on a large raised podium. Design your own roof, considering how the interior acoustics of the building might influence the external roof shape.

Design a roof form that could be supported by this podium...

The Sydney Opera House, Sydney, Australia. Jørn Utzon, 1973

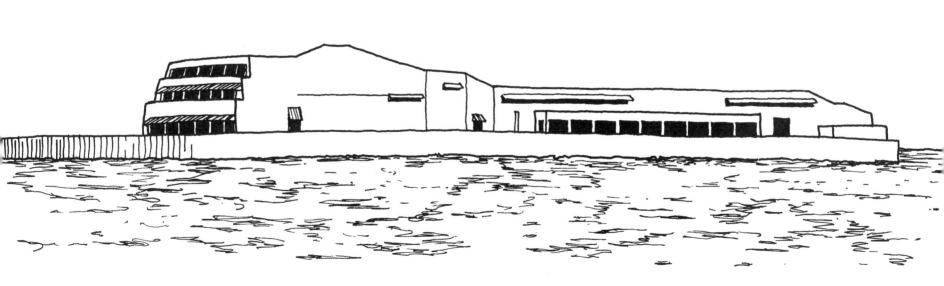

Characterized by their **symbolic roof forms,**
representing equilibrium and balance, the civic buildings for Brazil's new capital
Brasília were designed by Oscar Niemeyer.

Make other suggestions of roof forms that would symbolize
Brazilian progress in the 21st century. ...

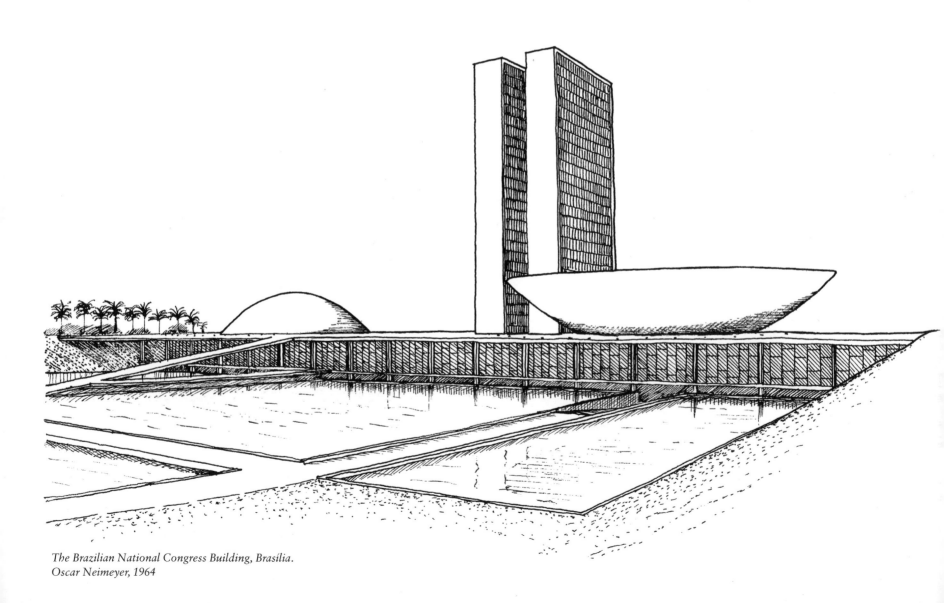

The Brazilian National Congress Building, Brasília.
Oscar Neimeyer, 1964

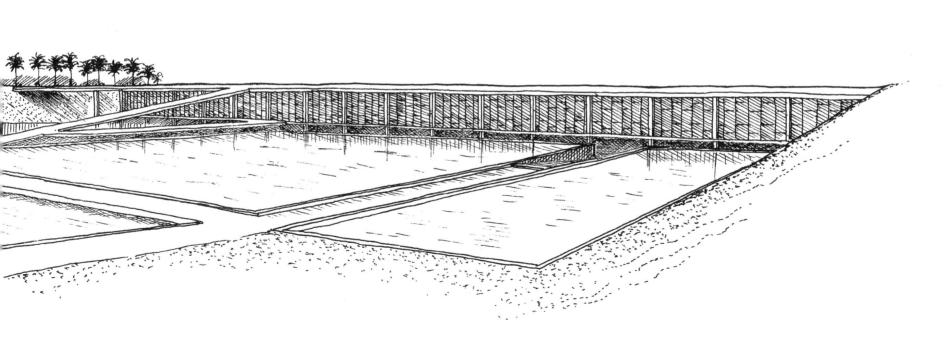

Austrian architectural group **Coop Himmelb(l)au** often begin projects with an intuitive sketch that they describe as 'draw[ing] with one's eyes closed', akin to the 'automatic drawing' practised by Dadaists and Surrealists. This rooftop extension is an example of this method.

Make your own 'automatic drawing' and use it to generate the plan or section of a building. You may need to make a sketch model first...

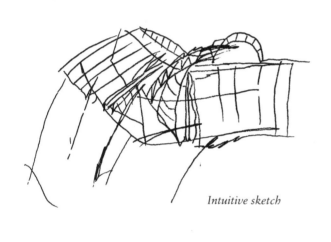

Intuitive sketch

Falkestrasse rooftop renovation, Vienna, Austria. Coop Himmelb(l)au, 1988

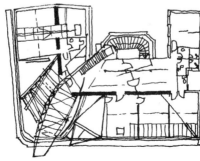

Plan drawing

Populating planets
has long been a dream of man as he has explored the outer reaches of space.

Design a new zero-gravity community for the surface of Titan...

The **De Stijl** (the Style) movement in the Netherlands began in 1917, its work characterized by abstract composition and strong primary colours. The most famous exponents of De Stijl were Piet Mondrian, Gerrit Rietveld and Theo van Doesburg.

Design a kiosk to sell the De Stijl *magazine and express the spirit of the movement...*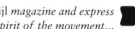

Drawing of the typeface created by van Doesburg for the De Stijl *magazine*

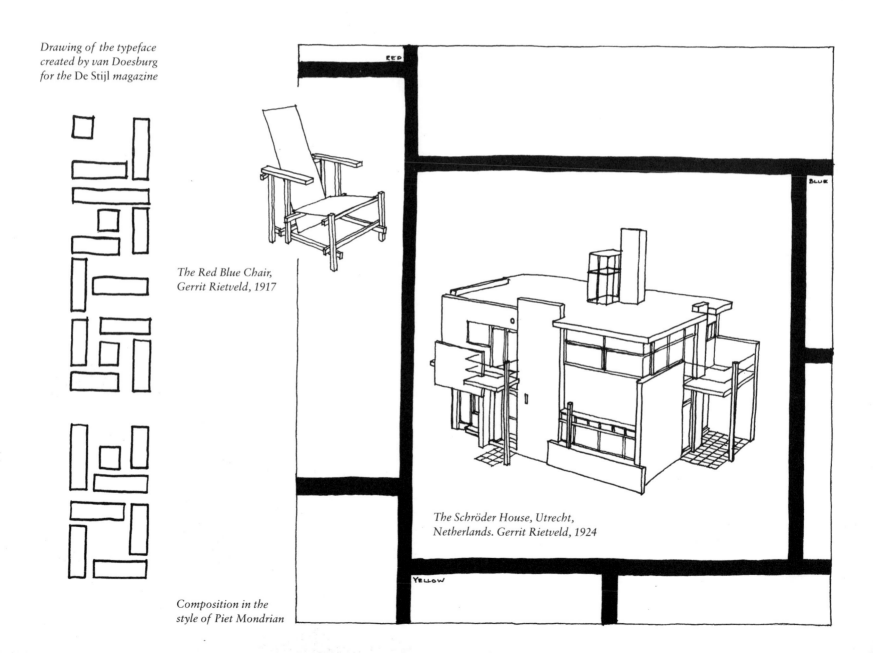

The Red Blue Chair, Gerrit Rietveld, 1917

The Schröder House, Utrecht, Netherlands. Gerrit Rietveld, 1924

Composition in the style of Piet Mondrian

Design for a Kiosk,
Lajos Kassák, 1923

Many architects have designed very distinctive and important **chairs** using lots of different shapes and sizes.

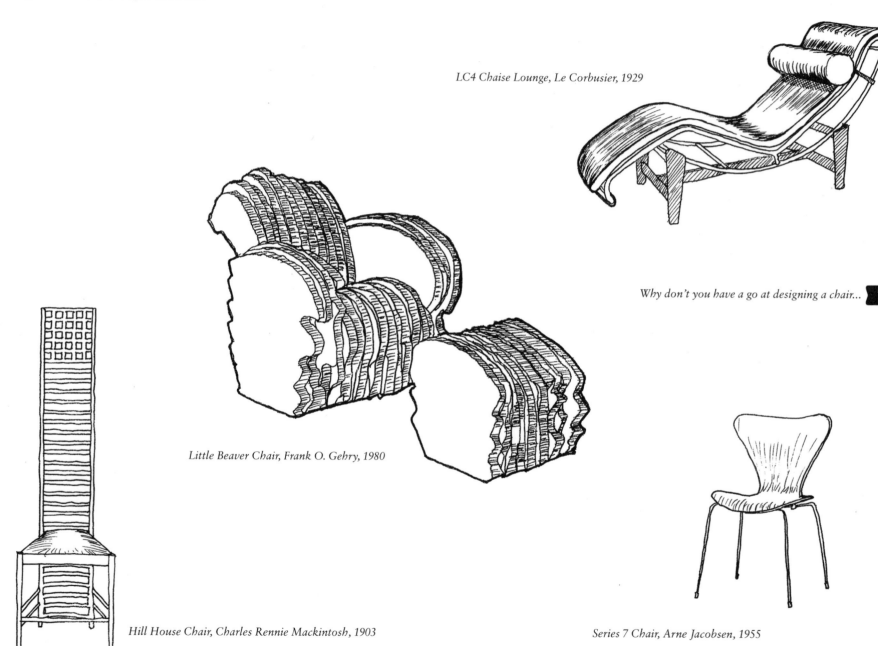

LC4 Chaise Lounge, Le Corbusier, 1929

Why don't you have a go at designing a chair...

Little Beaver Chair, Frank O. Gehry, 1980

Hill House Chair, Charles Rennie Mackintosh, 1903

Series 7 Chair, Arne Jacobsen, 1955

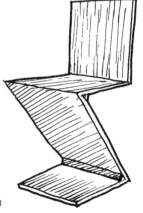

Zig Zag Chair, Gerrit Rietveld, 1934

...you may also consider a **design for seating**
for more than one person.

Monte Carlo Sofa, Eileen Gray, 1929

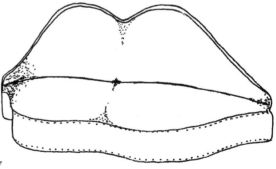

Mae West Lips Sofa, Salvador Dalí, 1937

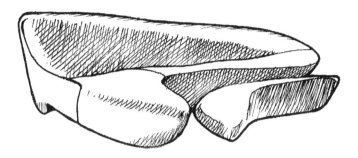

Moon System sofa, Zaha Hadid, 2007

Pantower, Verner Panton, 1969

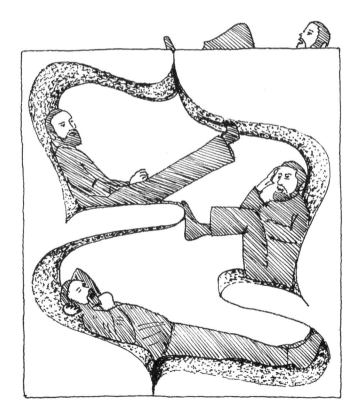

Here are a variety of things to consider when **designing a window** and its opening.

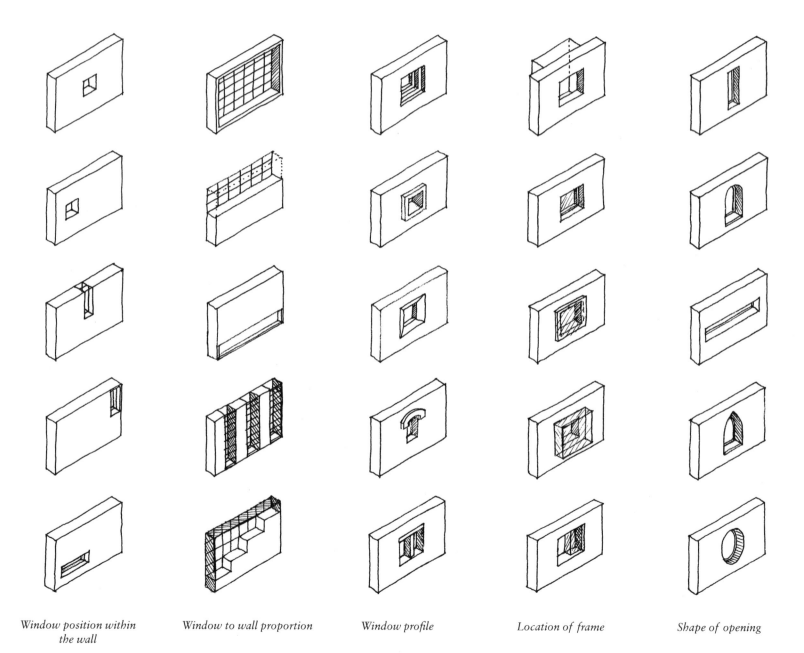

| Window position within the wall | Window to wall proportion | Window profile | Location of frame | Shape of opening |

an you suggest any more variations?

Each of these buildings has a different attitude to **window design**:
projecting bay, window wall, free-form hole.

Suggest some other types of window openings...

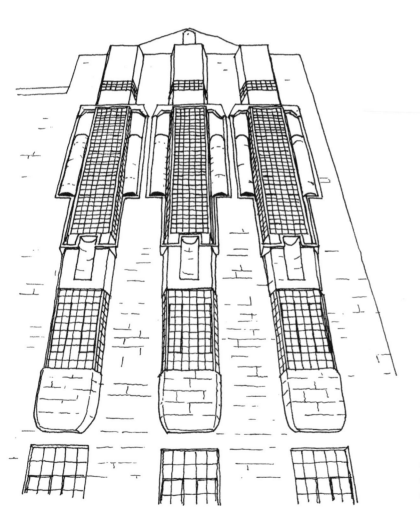

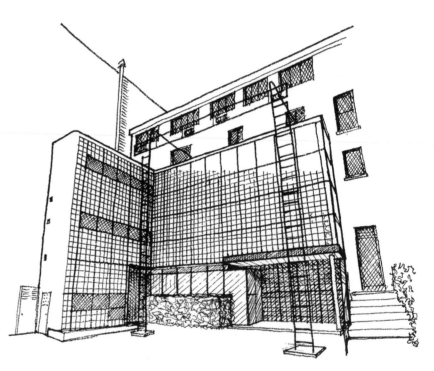

Maison de Verre, Paris, France. Pierre Chareau and Bernard Bijvoet, 1932

Glasgow School of Art, Scotland. Charles Rennie Mackintosh, 1909

The Public arts building,
West Midlands, England.
Will Alsop, 2008

Different **types and shapes of window** make up the façade of this
building: recessed (circular), flush (oblong), projecting (square) and clerestory (below the roofline; horizontal).

*Using the same exterior wall, experiment with your own
composition of windows and openings...*

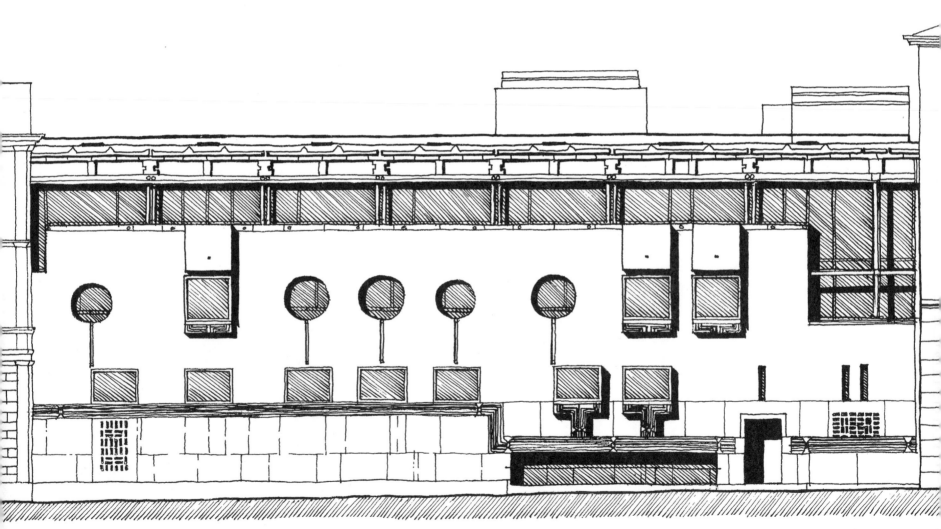

Banca Popolare di Verona, Italy. Carlo Scarpa, 1973

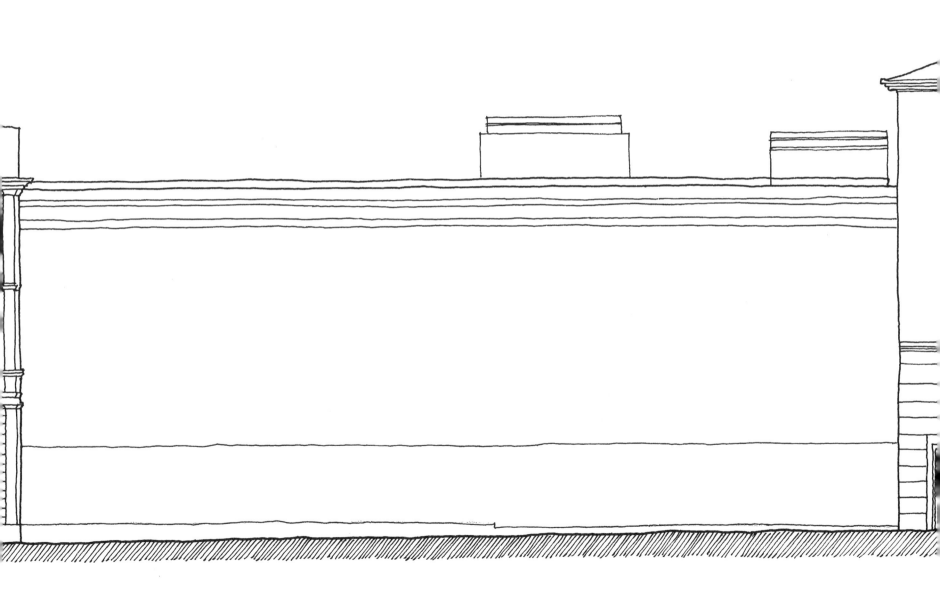

These innovative **beach huts** were created for a competition to 'Re-imagine the Beach Hut for the 21st Century'.

Considering seaside themes, what would your competition entry look like...

'Eyes Wide sHut', Feix&Merlin

'Alien Drum Sensorium', Alasdair Toozer, Gareth Hoskins Architects

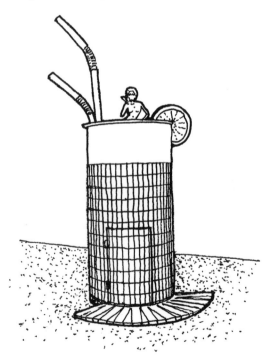

'Come Up and See Me', Michael Trainor

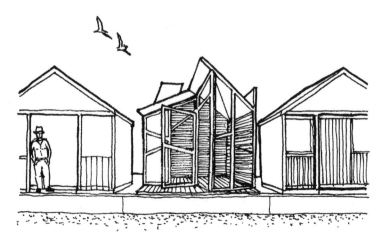

'Lattice Hut', Andrew Siddall, Civic Architects

'Cheese 42', Christian Uhl Architekt

Here is a street that is in desperate need of **'greening'.** Use some of the elements below to improve it.

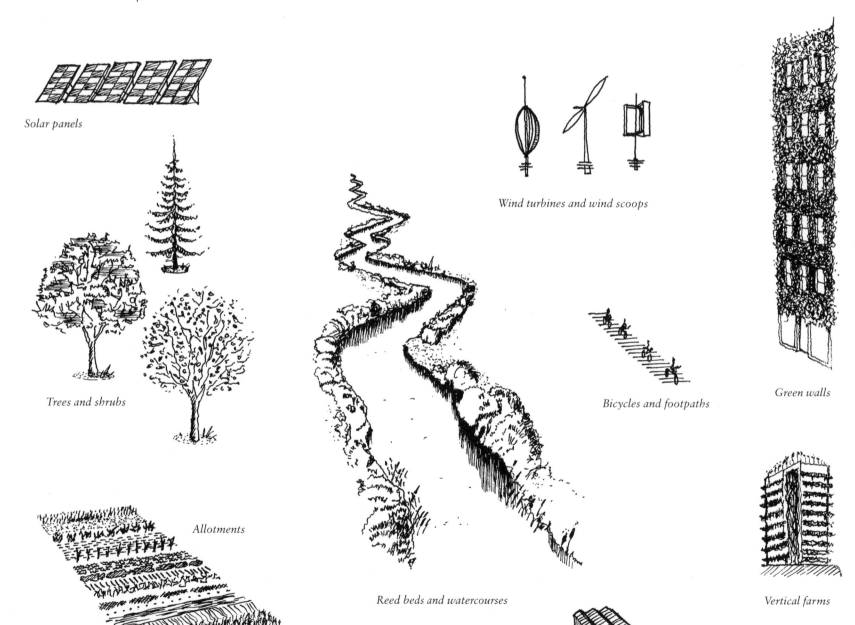

Solar panels

Trees and shrubs

Allotments

Reed beds and watercourses

Wind turbines and wind scoops

Bicycles and footpaths

Green walls

Greenhouses

Vertical farms

These buildings have all used **recycled materials**
to construct the fabric of the building.

'Pavilion of Temporary Happiness'
(33,000 beer crates), Brussels, Belgium.
SHSH Architecture/V+, 2008

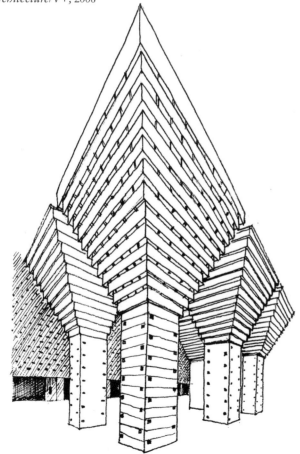

Manifesto House, (timber pallets), Curacaví,
Chile. James & Mau for Infiniski, 2009

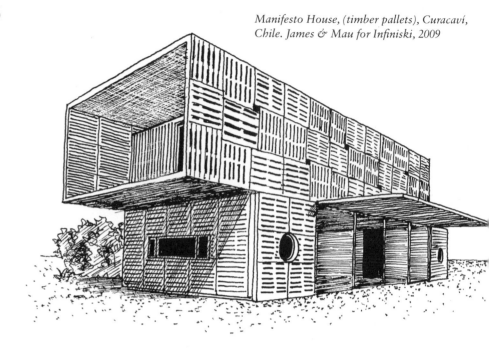

Sketch out the design of a simple house or pavilion using waste products...

Lucy's House (27,000 stacked carpet tiles), Alabama,
USA. Samuel Mockbee, Rural Studio, 1997

Wat Pa Maha Chedi Kaew temple (1.5 million beer bottles), Sisaket province, Thailand.

The **Bauhaus** school of design, founded in Germany in 1919, took a radical approach to the combined teaching of craft and design with the ambition of creating a new unity between art and technology. They explored the new techniques of industrialization through simple geometric forms.

Create your own sculptural form using a combination of circles, triangles and squares...

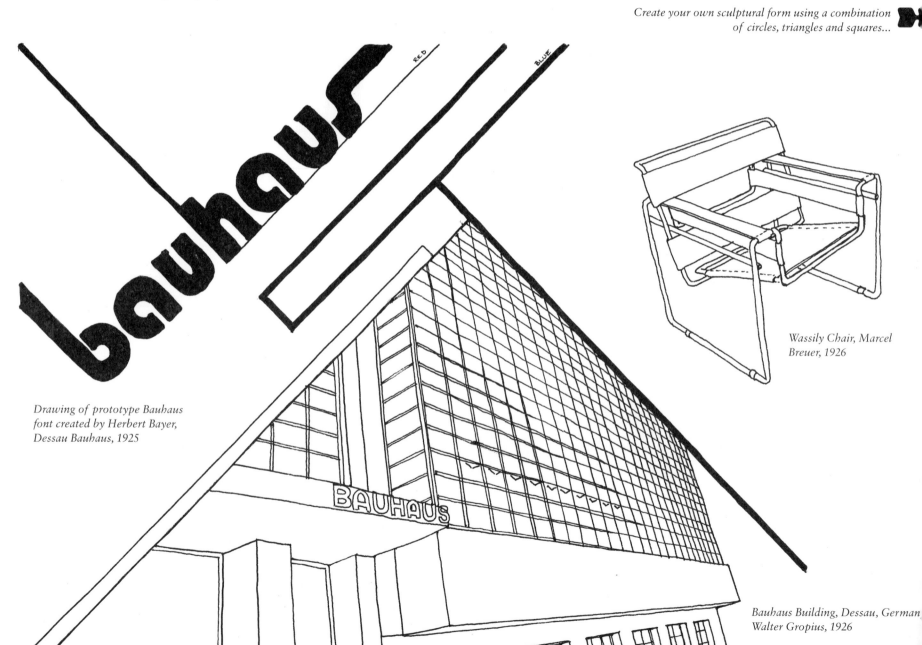

Drawing of prototype Bauhaus font created by Herbert Bayer, Dessau Bauhaus, 1925

Wassily Chair, Marcel Breuer, 1926

Bauhaus Building, Dessau, German Walter Gropius, 1926

Monument to the March Dead, Weimar, Germany. Walter Gropius, 1922

Here are a various **wall structures**.

Thin Plane   *Battered*   *Close Column*   *Mass*   *Masonry*

Thick Plane   *Stepped*   *Log Wall*   *Frame*   *Timber*

Honeycomb   *Parallel Plane*   *Fabric Skin*   *In Fill*   *Concrete*

Buttress   *Panel*   *Pneumatic Air*   *Layered*   *Glass*

Crenulated   *Corrugated*   *Plastic*   *Woven*   *Metal*

Design some walls of your own, taking into consideration their construction and material...

Sculptural curvilinear walls of different thickness, topped off
with a heavy overhanging roof, characterize the design of the Chapel of Notre Dame du Haut.

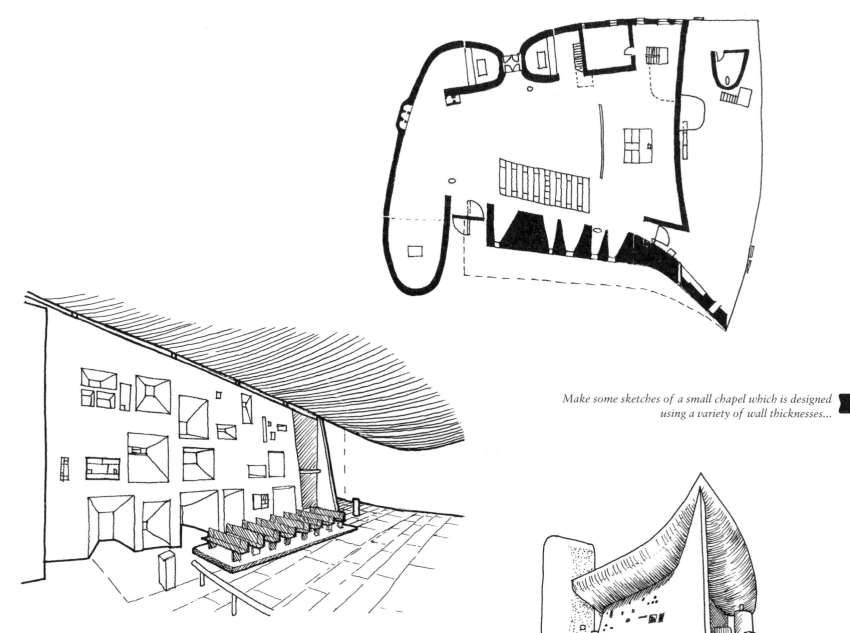

*Make some sketches of a small chapel which is designed
using a variety of wall thicknesses...*

*The Chapel of Notre Dame du Haut, Ronchamp,
France. Le Corbusier, 1954*

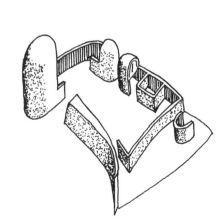

'A House is a Machine for Living in'
— Le Corbusier

Design and draw the sectional view of a house that has been influenced by a machine...

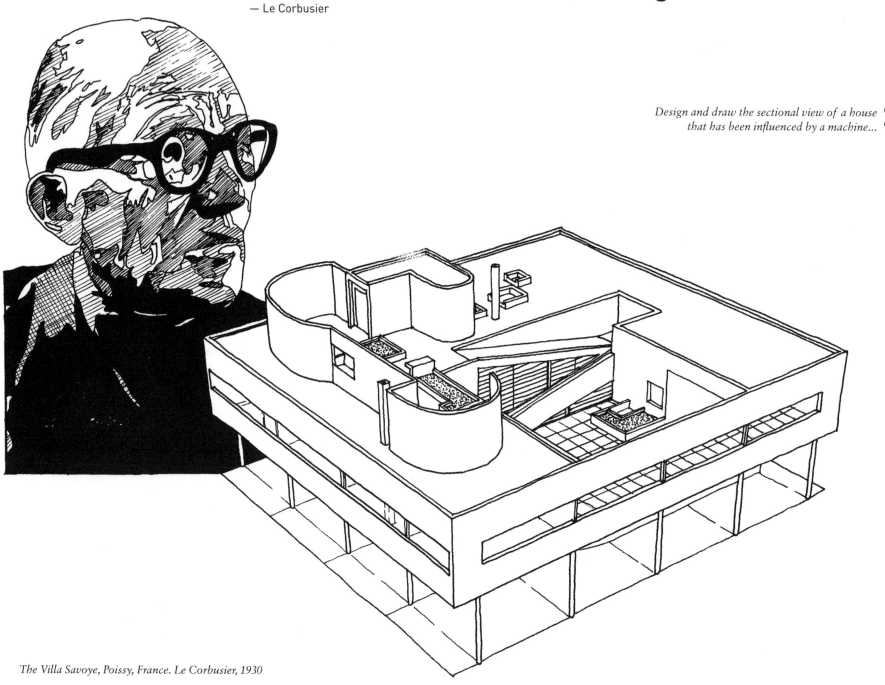

The Villa Savoye, Poissy, France. Le Corbusier, 1930

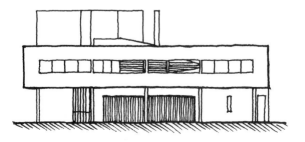

The five **columns** shown here represent the principal orders of classical architecture – Tuscan, Doric, Ionic, Corinthian and Composite.

Design your own column...

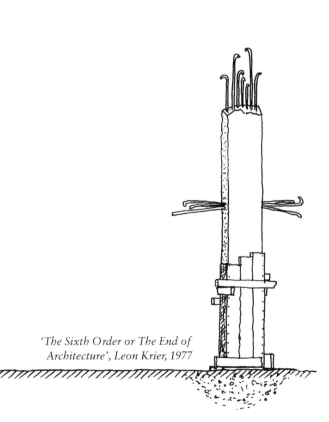

'The Sixth Order or The End of
Architecture', Leon Krier, 1977

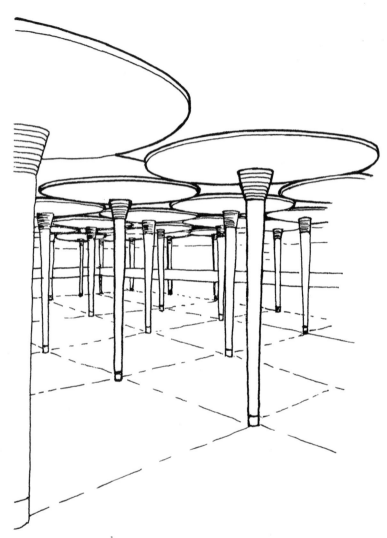

Here are some **contemporary columns** that
articulate how the load is transferred from the roof to the base. Try some for yourself

Johnson Wax Administration Building, Wisconsin, USA.
Frank Lloyd Wright, 1939

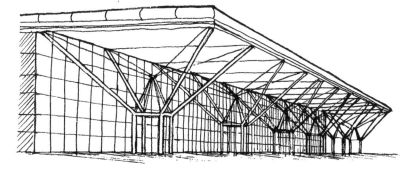

Stansted Airport, London, England. Foster+Partners, 1991

These examples show **columns and beams** expressed as one element. What ideas can you develop?

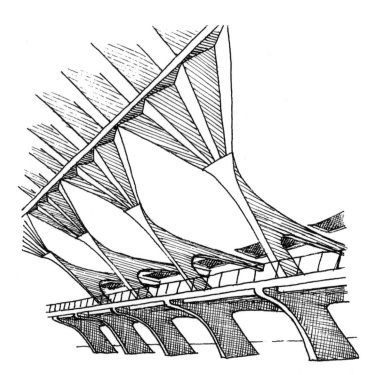

Exhibition Hall, Turin, Italy. Pier Luigi Nervi, 1949

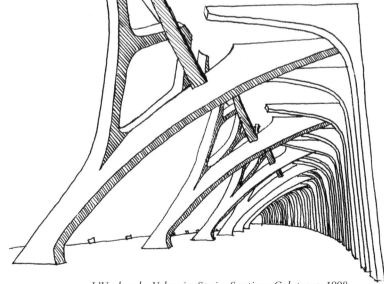

L'Umbracle, Valencia, Spain. Santiago Calatrava, 1998

This copy of a comparative study of how one might resolve a **corner house** was drawn by the Luxembourgian architect Rob Krier.

See how many more variations you can add to the 24 shown here...

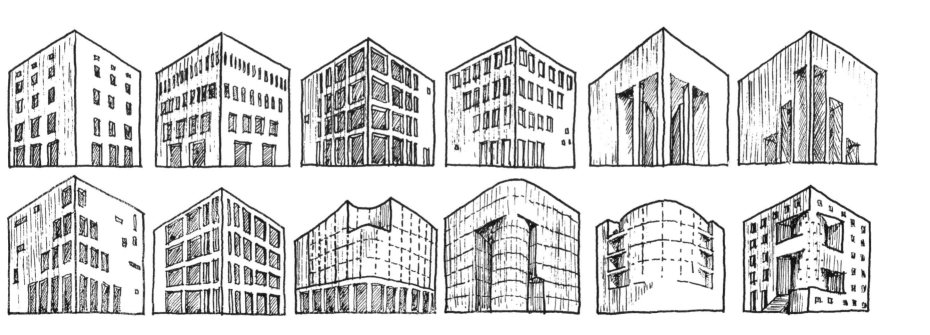

Kinetic buildings 1: The Sliding House by dRMM

Architects has a timber skin that can be slid off to reveal a transparent layer underneath. This skin is on tracks, powered by PV solar panels, and can be moved to enjoy maximum sunlight and then retracted to retain the heat.

Design a simple structure that interacts with the sun... ▶

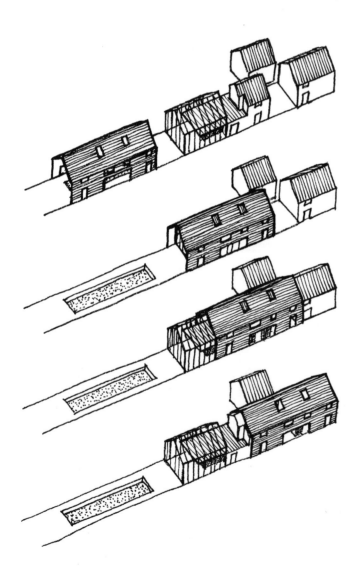

Sliding House, Suffolk, England. dRMM Architects, 2009

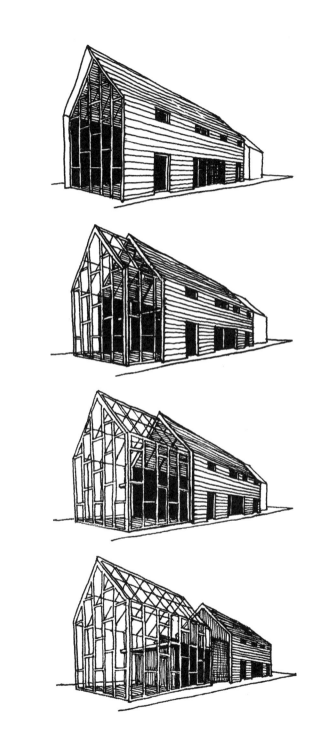

Kinetic buildings 2: Here is an example of a building

that is 'in a state of permanent transformation'. Its concept is that of a simple timber box that folds open and reveals its interior. The 'GucklHupf' is used as a contemplative space as well as a place for musical performances and poetry readings.

Design your own performance space using the same principles of hinging and folding...

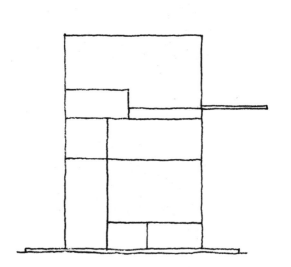 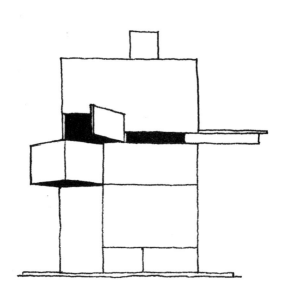 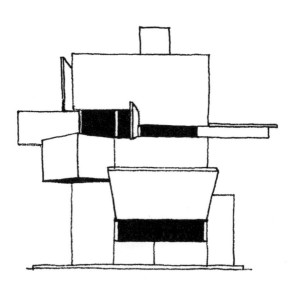

GucklHupf, Mondsee, Austria. Hans Peter Wörndl, 1993

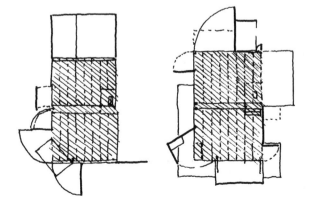

Plan drawings

The Triangular Lodge

is a folly, and its design was a reflection of the architect's Roman Catholic faith, the number three symbolizing the Holy Trinity. This number is expressed throughout; there are three floors, three trefoil windows, three triangular gables on each side, a triangular plan, and so on.

Design your own folly based around a number, pattern, shape or proportional system...

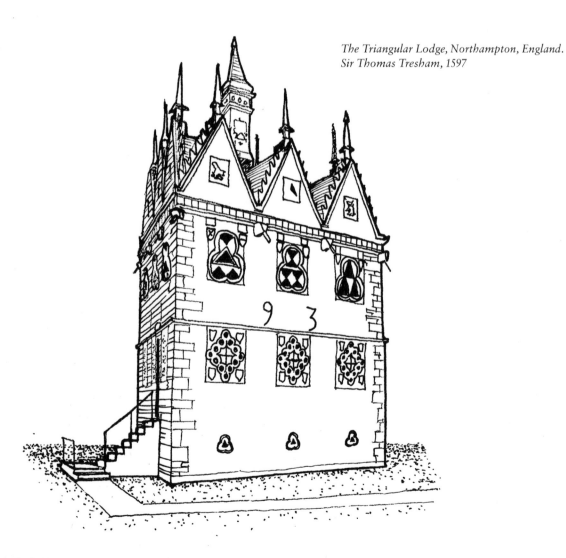

The Triangular Lodge, Northampton, England.
Sir Thomas Tresham, 1597

Plan drawing

The design of one of the largest parks in Paris has many **follies** laid out in a grid. The 35 follies were the architect's device for organizing and orientating visitors within the landscape. The follies were designed in the form of partly open red frameworks, waiting for both functions and events to inhabit the spaces within.

Design a modern folly using a framed grid as a starting point...

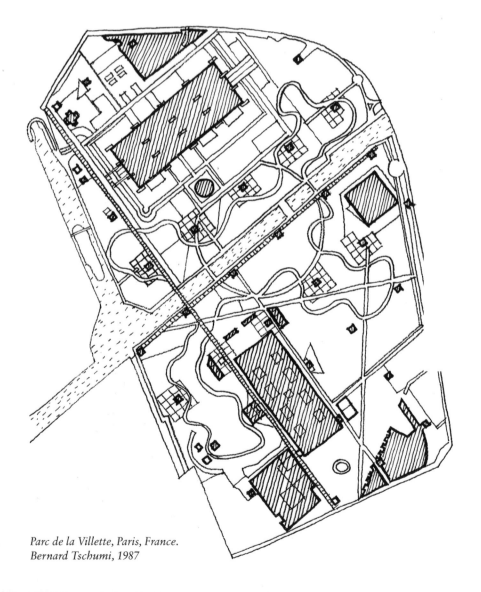

Parc de la Villette, Paris, France.
Bernard Tschumi, 1987

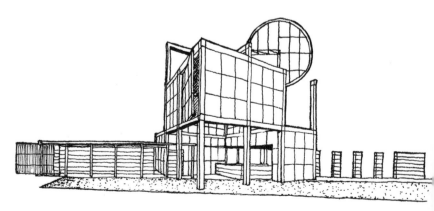

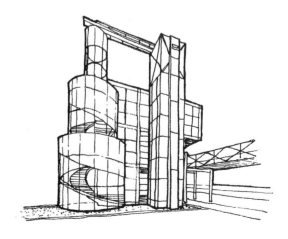

Here are some examples of unusual **tree houses.**

Draw the rest of the forest and locate the design of your tree house within it...

Ecocoons, Mathieu Collos, 2009

*Takasugi-an Tea House, Ja
Terunobu Fujimori, 2004*

Yellow Treehouse, Auckland, New Zealand. Pacific Environments Architects, 2009

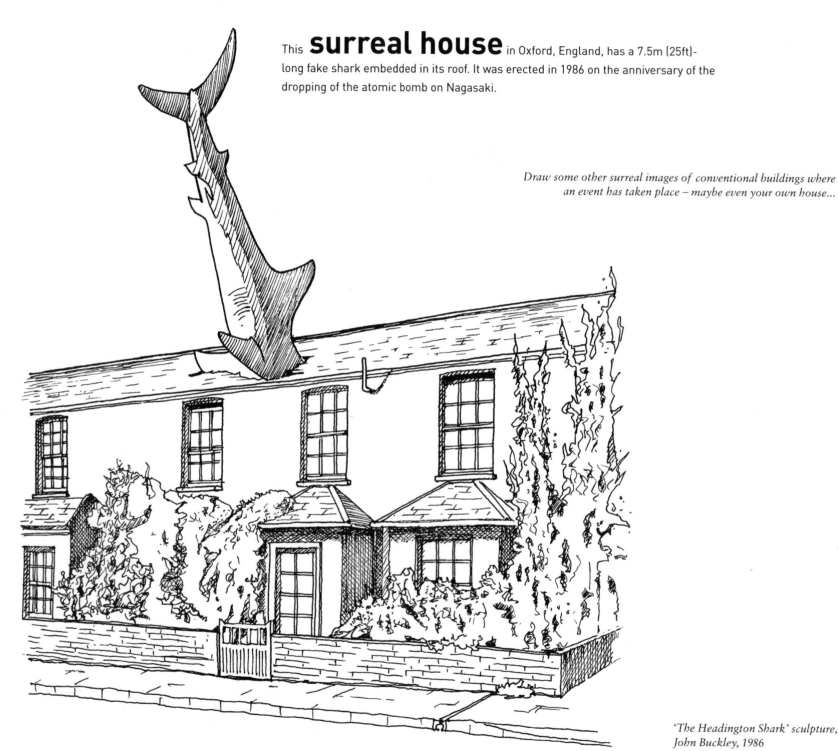

This **surreal house** in Oxford, England, has a 7.5m (25ft)-long fake shark embedded in its roof. It was erected in 1986 on the anniversary of the dropping of the atomic bomb on Nagasaki.

Draw some other surreal images of conventional buildings where an event has taken place – maybe even your own house...

'The Headington Shark' sculpture, John Buckley, 1986

The Airplane Hotel, Costa Rica,
Costa Verde, 2010

Your wealthy client wants to build a house on his **private island** but he's not sure where to build it. Think about what would be a good view, and which direction the sun and wind come from.

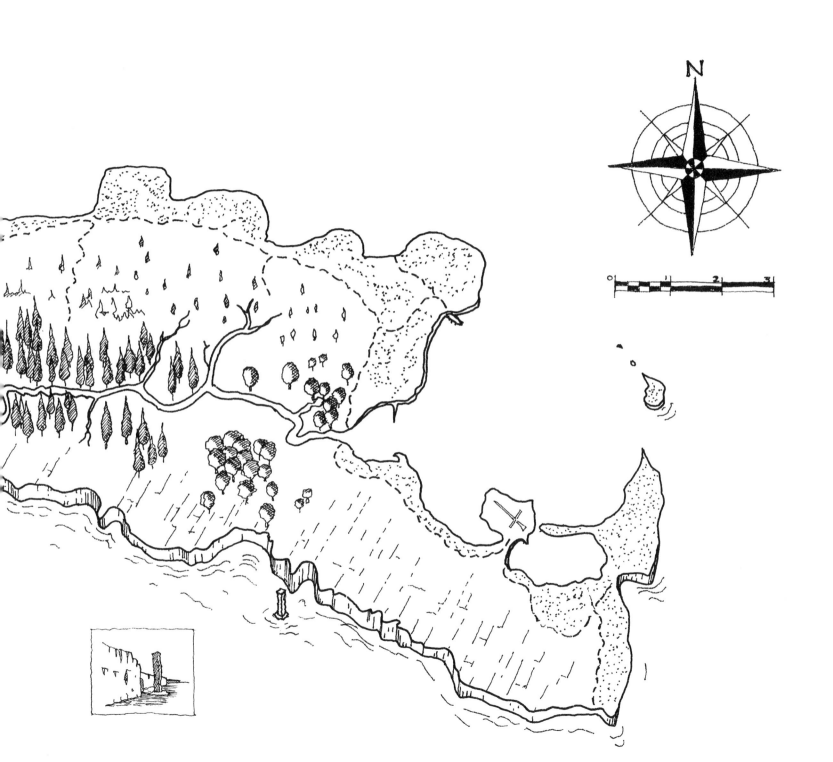

Design a house on a cliff...

and by a waterfall...

Draw a house by a river...

in the mountains...

The **Constructivist** movement emerged in Russia after the 1917 Revolution. Its aim was to create an aesthetic that reflected the new industrial power of the country. Monuments like the 'Tatlin Tower' were designed using steel to celebrate 20th-century industrialization.

Design a new monument for the 21st century using materials and forms that reflect current ideas...

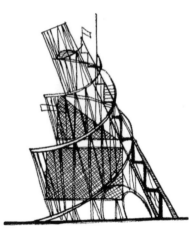

The Monument to the Third Internation Vladimir Tatlin, 1919

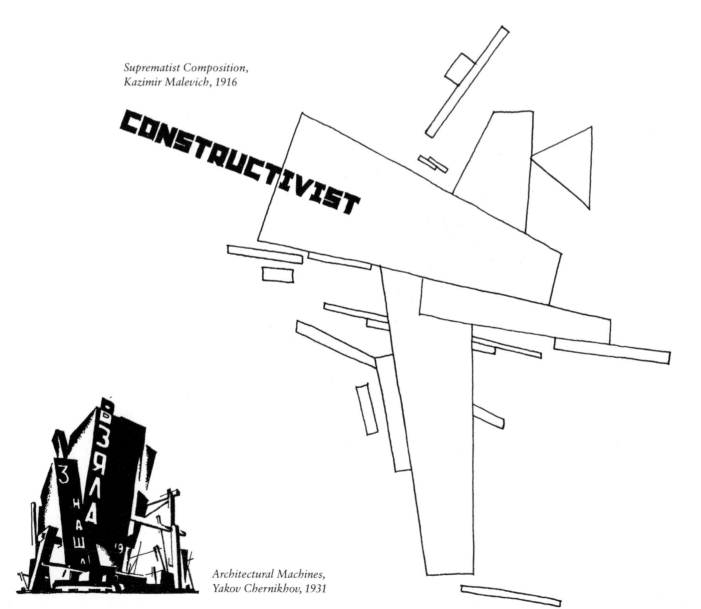

Suprematist Composition, Kazimir Malevich, 1916

Architectural Machines, Yakov Chernikhov, 1931

Lenin Tribune, El Lissitzsky, 1920

Complete the drawings of the following **iconic buildings...**

St Paul's Cathedral, London,
England. Sir Christopher Wren, 1710

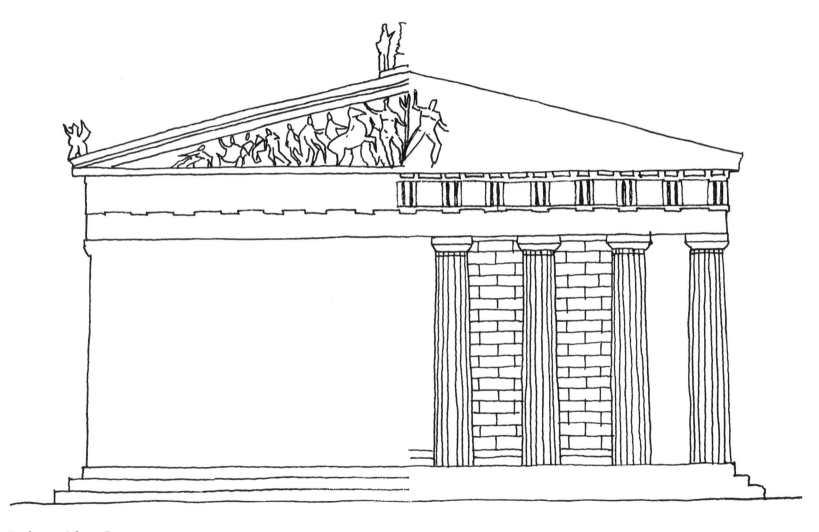

Parthenon, Athens, Greece.
Iktinos and Kallikrates, 432BC

The idea of **'servant' and 'served'** spaces in buildings was developed by the American architect Louis Kahn in the 1950s. Kahn studied Scottish castles, discovering that minor spaces – stairs and areas for cooking and washing, etc. – were contained within the walls and were like servants to the major communal 'served' areas.

Colour in the servant spaces on these plans of four buildings by Louis Kahn. Try to identify 'servant' and 'served' spaces in other buildings...

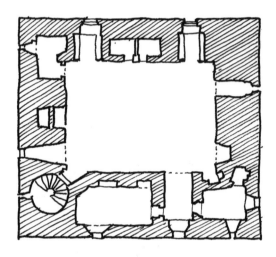

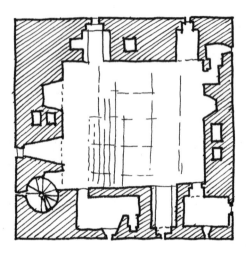

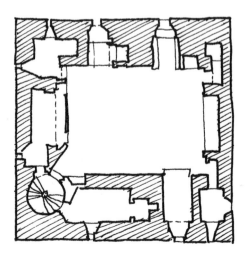

Trenton Bath House, 1955

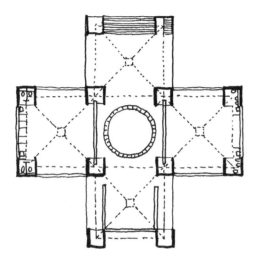

Yale Center for British Art, 1974

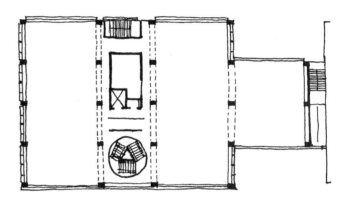

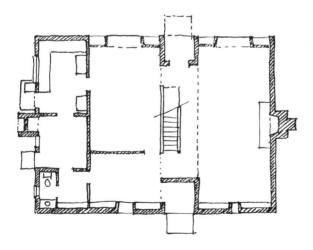

Esherick House, 1961

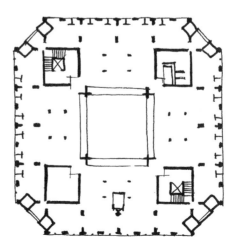

Phillips Exeter Academy Library, 1971

Many famous architects wear **glasses.**

Johnson

Le Corbusier

Sejima

Libeskind

Gehry

Design a new piece of face furniture for yourself.
Cut them out, mount them on card and wear them before
taking on the next task...

You have been appointed to **design a 'new look'**
for Buckingham Palace, the London residence of the Queen of England.

Using this outline drawing as a background, create your new design...

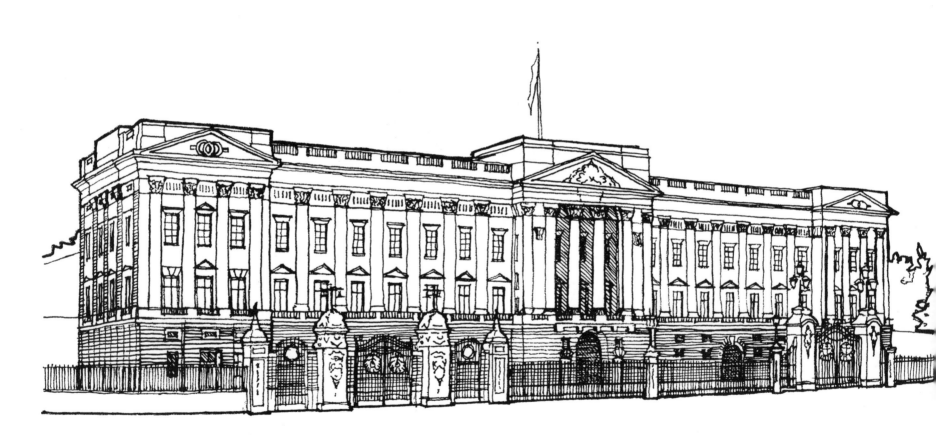

*Buckingham Palace, The City of Westminster,
England. John Nash, 1820s*

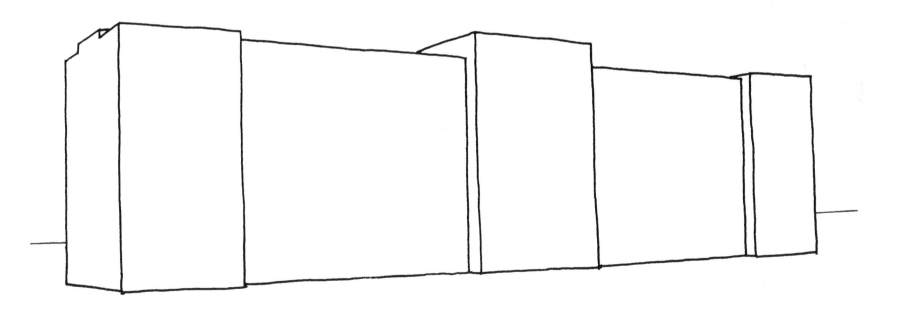

Buildings are either a **duck or decorated shed**
according to architects Robert Venturi, Denise Scott Brown and Steven Izenour in their 1972
book *Learning from Las Vegas*. A 'duck' (named after a duck-shaped building that sold eggs
in New York) is a building whose form tells us what its purpose is. A 'decorated shed', on the
other hand, is generic in shape and can only be identified by its signage and decoration.

Draw your own 'duck' and 'decorated shed' buildings,
indicating what they are by shape or by the use of signage...

The Big Duck, Flanders, New York,
USA, 1931

The Golden Nugget Casino, Las Vegas, USA, 1946

Copy of a sketch 'I am a Monument',
by Venturi and Scott Brown, 1972

Modern **sports stadia** provide good examples of a 'Duck' or 'Decorated Shed'. However, sometimes they can be read as both. So are the stadia shown here 'ducks' or 'decorated sheds' or both?

Sketch some ideas for a sports stadium with this notion in mind...

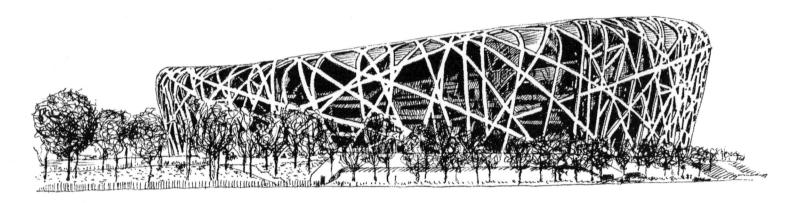

National Stadium (known as the 'Bird's Nest'), Beijing, China.
Herzog and de Meuron, 2008

Stadio San Nicola, Bari, Italy.
Renzo Piano, 1990

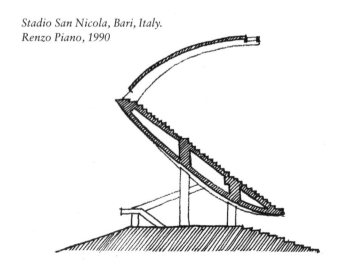

Proposed National Stadium, Japan,
Zaha Hadid, 2019

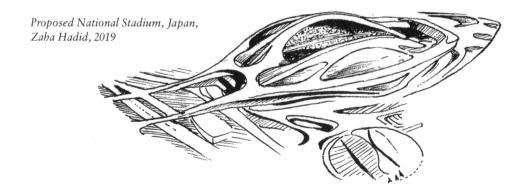

Allianz Arena, Munich, Germany.
Herzog and de Meuron, 2005

'Less is More'
— Ludwig Mies van der Rohe

Design your own minimal house...

*The Farnsworth House, Piano, Illinois.
Ludwig Mies van der Rohe, 1951*

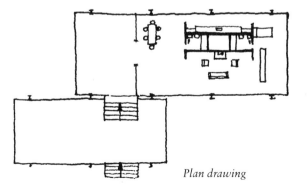

Plan drawing

Here is the plan of a house for the **Berlin Building Exhibition**
designed by Ludwig Mies van der Rohe and Lilly Reich in 1931.

*Using the drawing key of furniture and utilities, mark on the plan
the spaces where you would like to cook, eat, wash, sleep, study and relax…*

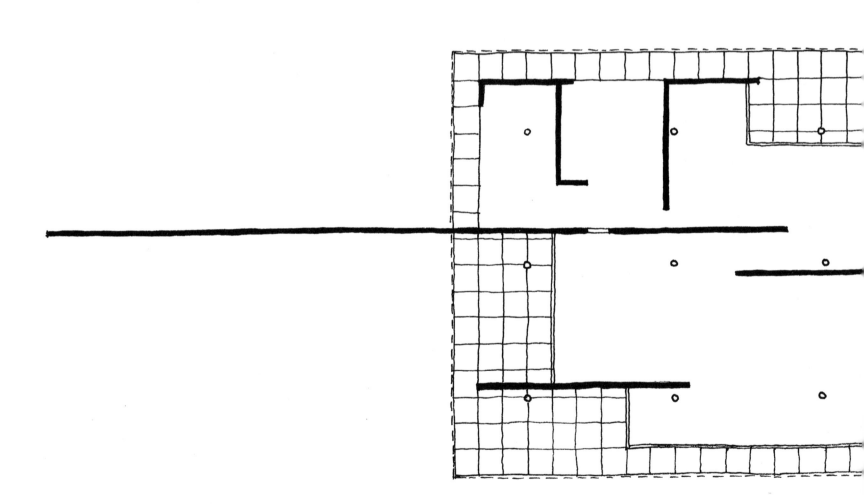

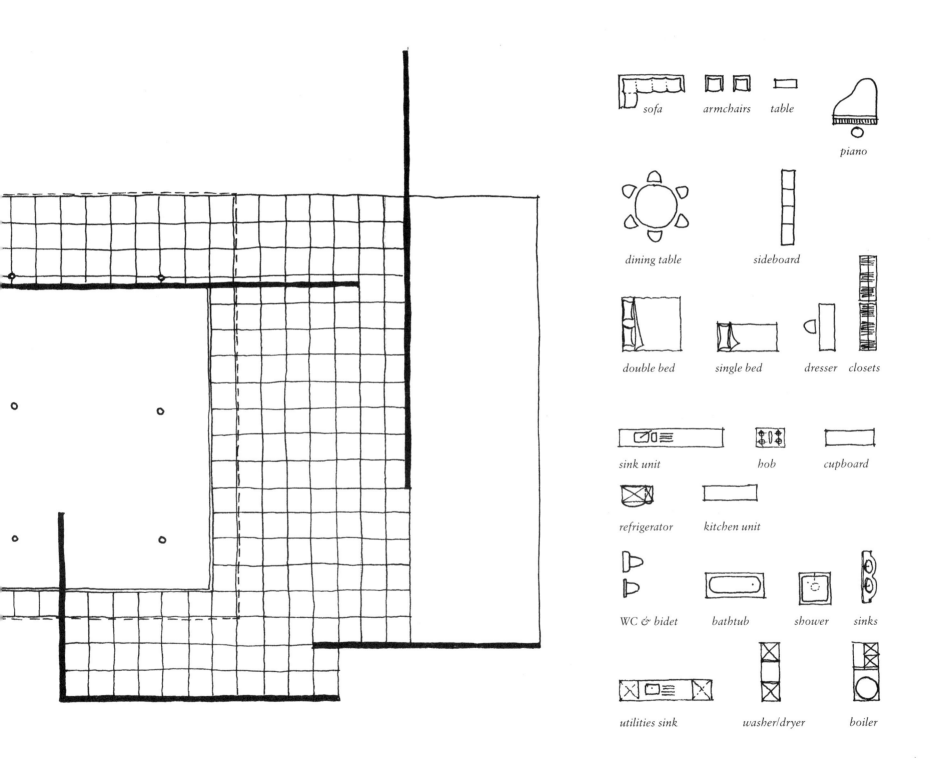

sofa　　*armchairs*　　*table*

piano

dining table　　　　*sideboard*

double bed　　*single bed*　　*dresser*　*closets*

sink unit　　　　*hob*　　　*cupboard*

refrigerator　　*kitchen unit*

WC & bidet　　*bathtub*　　*shower*　　*sinks*

utilities sink　　*washer/dryer*　　*boiler*

Here are some examples of **curvilinear stairs**.

Casa dels Ous, Torre de la Creu, Spain.
Josep Maria Jujol, 1916

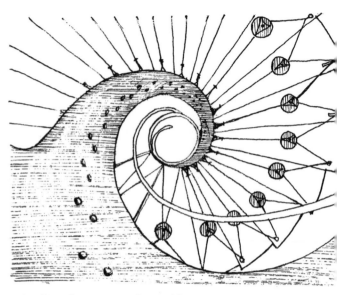

Hotel Josef, Prague, Czech Republic.
Eva Jiricna, 2002

Sketch some ideas for a stair which articulates
circles and curves within the design...

Louvre Pyramid, Paris, France.
I.M. Pei, 1989

These **innovative stairs** were designed for a London house and incorporate a bench next to the entrance and storage leading to a bed platform.

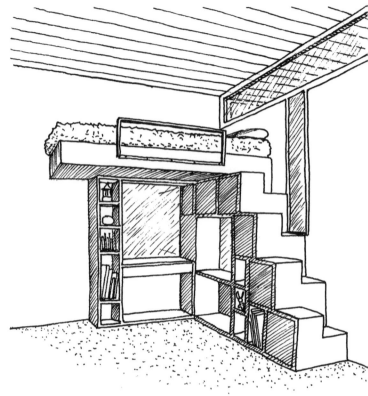

Town House, London, England.
Tankard Bowkett, 2001

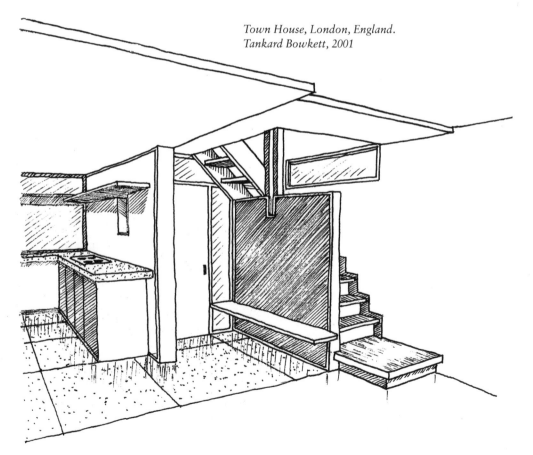

Sketch your own ideas for these two spaces...

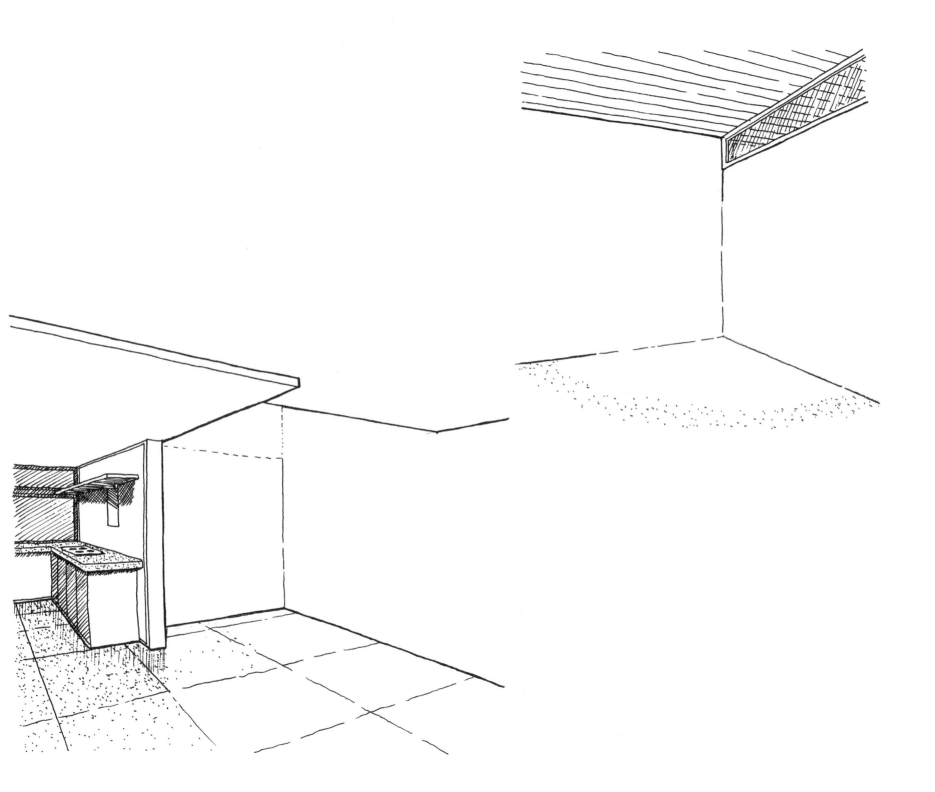

This **display staircase** appears to float within the space and provides a centre point for exhibiting artefacts in the Olivetti Showroom in Venice.

How would you design a stair for this space leading up the first-floor mezzanine?

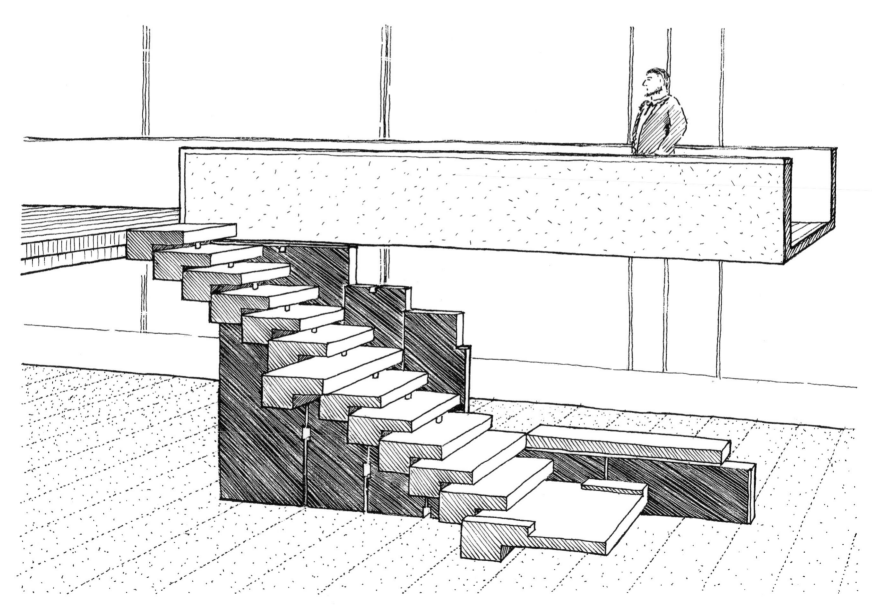

Olivetti Showroom Staircase, Venice, Italy. Carlo Scarpa, 1958.

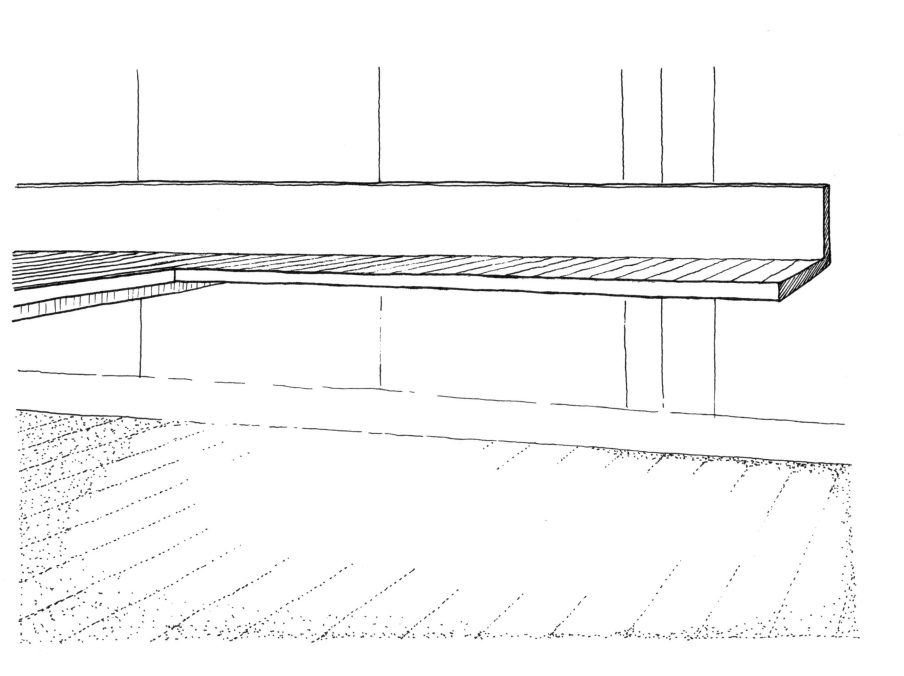

Atelier Bow-Wow Architects coined the term **'pet architecture'**
for small buildings built in the left over spaces next to big buildings. If this building, known
as 'the Gherkin', had a pet, would it be shaped like a pastrami sandwich? Or a mustard pot?

Choose a well-known building and design a 'pet' for it...

*30 St Mary Axe (the 'Gherkin'), London,
England. Norman Foster, 2003*

In 2004, architects **Tonkin Liu** designed and built a hill-top sound sculpture overlooking the town of Burnley in Lancashire, England. Their interactive design, the 'Singing Ringing Tree', was named after the Brothers Grimm folk story.

Design a sculptural form that interacts with the elements and think of a suitable title for it...

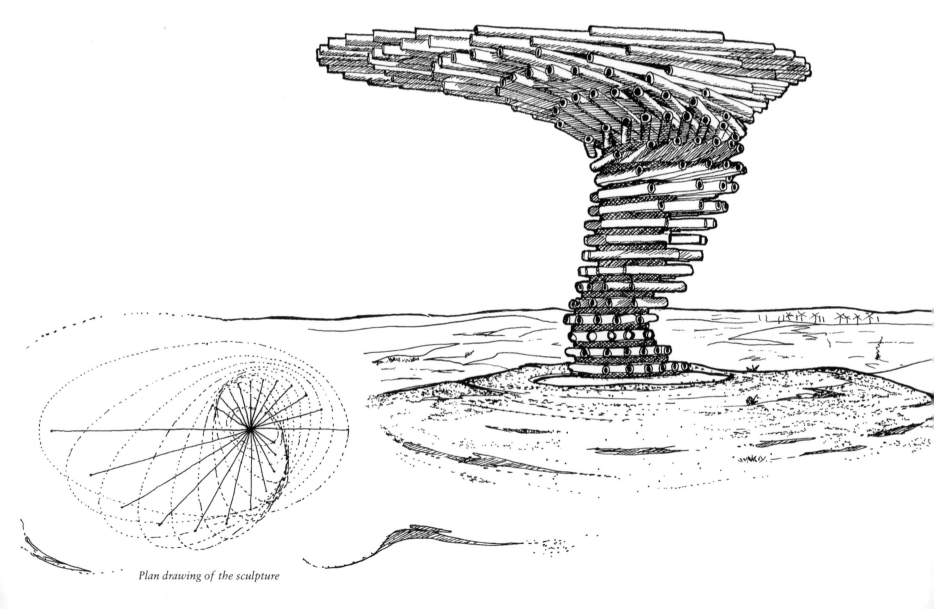

Plan drawing of the sculpture

Fluid and dynamic sketching is a style developed by the German Expressionist architect

Erich Mendelsohn. The sketch drawings of the Einstein Tower on the left show how the building form evolved.

Make some development sketches of a small tower of your own using a brush, ink and drawing pens...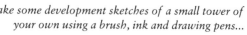

The Einstein Tower, Potsdam, Germany. Erich Mendelsohn, 1921

These are all examples of buildings with **unusual chimneys**.

Daneshill Brick and Tile Company, Hampshire, England. Sir Edwin Lutyens, 1903

Design a funky-looking chimney...

Das Heizhaus, Switzerland. Rudolf Steiner, 1914

Casa Milà, Barcelona, Spain. Antonio Gaudí, 1912

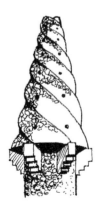

Palau Güell, Barcelona, Spain.
Antonio Gaudí, 1890

The **Borneo-Sporenburg** housing development in

Amsterdam, conceived of by West 8 Architects, invited a number of architects to
design terraced houses within a 5m (16ft)-wide and 12m (39ft)-long plot.

*Using the gaps provided, design and draw your ideas for
the façades of new houses facing the canal...*

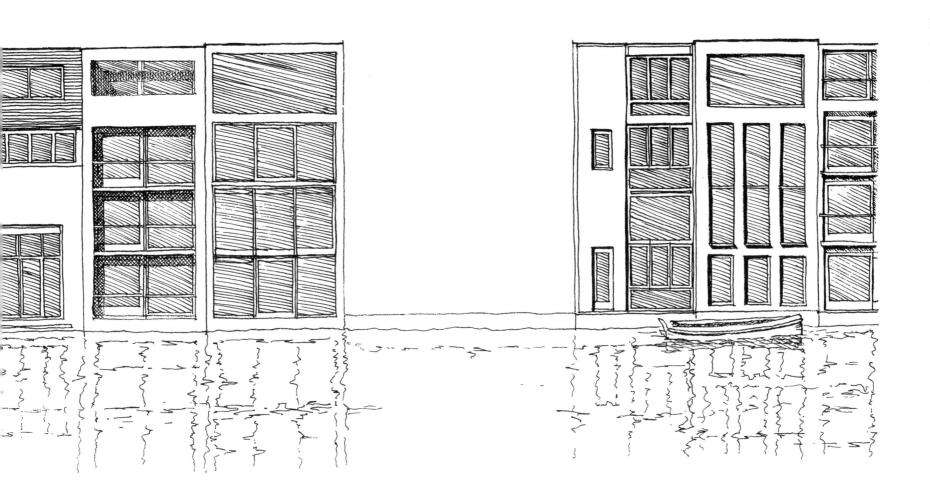

This **spiral-shaped house,** designed by the American architect Bruce Goff, is a dwelling that brings plants, pools and the surrounding countryside into the interior.

Design a house based upon a spiral form...

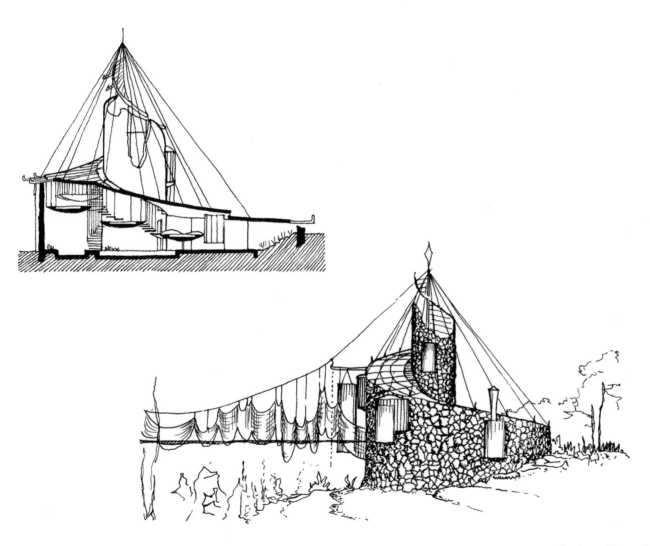

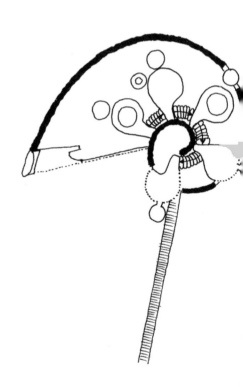

Bavinger House, Oklahoma, USA. Bruce Goff, 1955

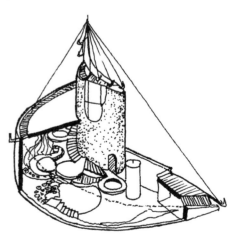

The **entrance** is a major consideration when designing a building. This threshold not only provides a way into an interior space but can also signify shelter, security, function, importance and opulence.

Schullin Jewellery Shop, Vienna, Austria. Hans Hollein, 1974

Sketch and design a new entrance for a building near you...

*Castel Béranger, Paris, France.
Hector Guimard, 1898*

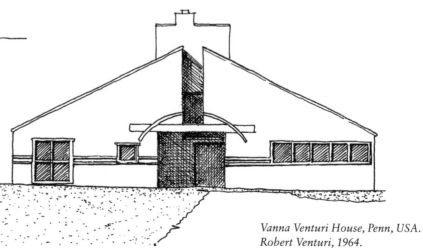

*Vanna Venturi House, Penn, USA.
Robert Venturi, 1964.*

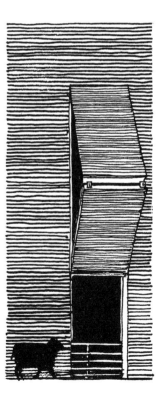

Petting Farm, Almere, the Netherlands.
70F Architecture, 2008

When designing a **door handle,** careful consideration should be given to comfort, material, strength and style.

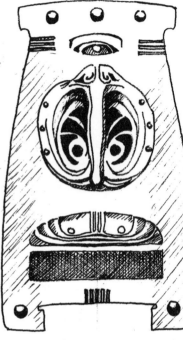

Art Nouveau door handle and letterbox, Brussels

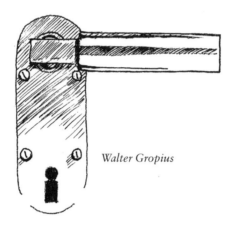

Walter Gropius

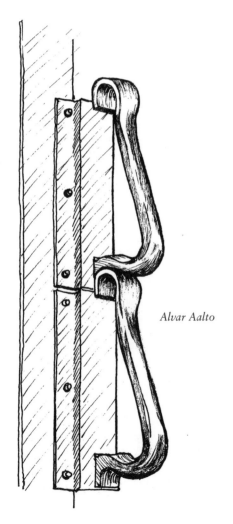

Alvar Aalto

Sketch a variety of door handle designs for different situations...

Alvar Aalto

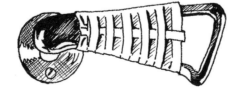

Zaha Hadid

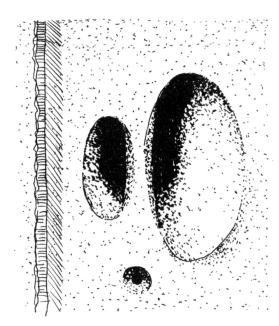

Peter Zumthor

Many architects have dedicated their time to designing **buildings for animals.**

Choose a creature from the animal kingdom and design a new dwelling for them...

The Penguin Pool, London Zoo, London. Berthold Lubetkin's Tecton Architectural Group, 1934

Gut Garkau Farm, Germany. Hugo Häring, 192●

The Savannah House, Rotterdam Zoo, the Netherlands. LAM Architects, 2009

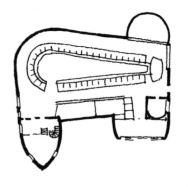

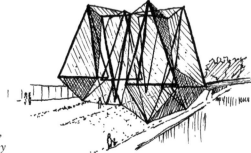

The Snowdon Aviary, London Zoo, England. Cedric Price, Frank Newby and Anthony Armstrong Jones, 1964

This **square house** was designed by American architect Charles Moore for himself. Made from timber, its design is based upon a series of squares within squares.

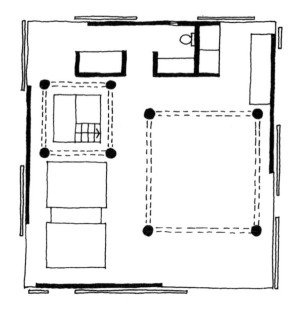

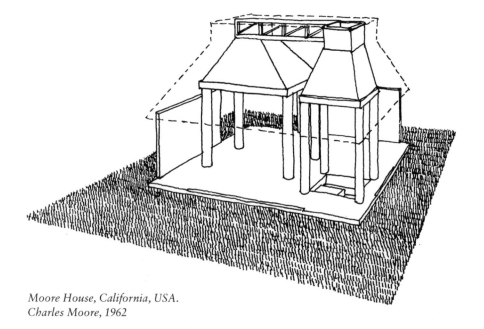

Moore House, California, USA.
Charles Moore, 1962

Design a small holiday home based upon square geometry...

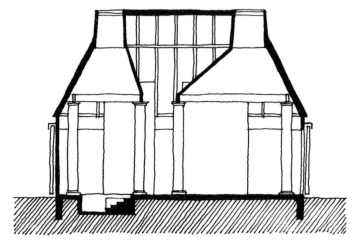

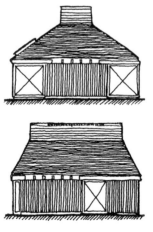

Architects have always been fascinated by exploring **rhythm and repetition** within the design of their buildings. These two examples of libraries by Finnish architect Alvar Aalto show how he changed the geometry between the fan-shaped reading areas and the rectilinear administration areas.

Sketch out some ideas for a small public library and show how you would exploit this principle....

Rovaniemi Library, Finland.
Alvar Aalto, 1965

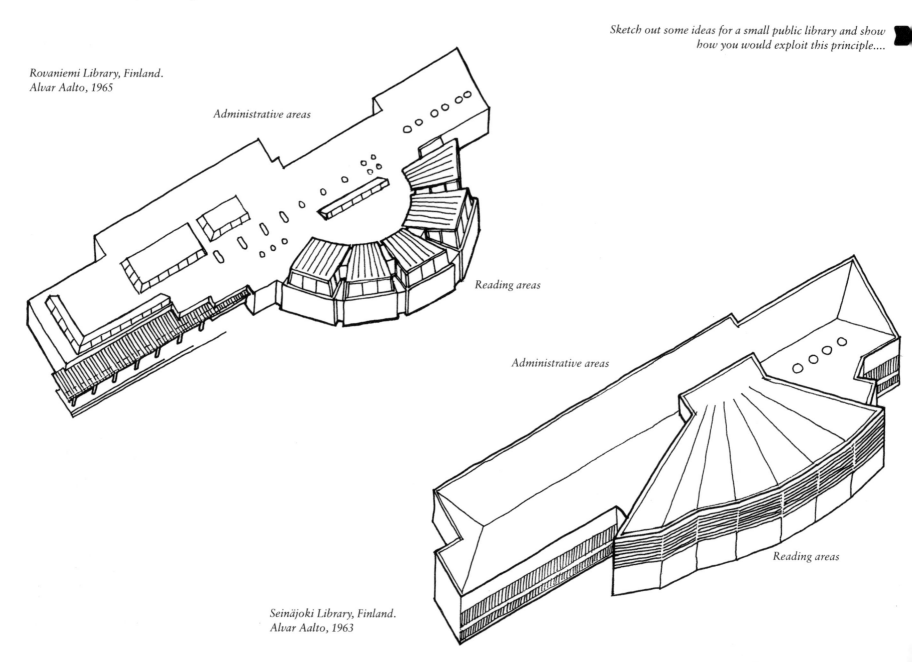

Administrative areas

Reading areas

Administrative areas

Reading areas

Seinäjoki Library, Finland.
Alvar Aalto, 1963

*Diagram showing principles
of rhythm and repetition*

Imagine if the owners of the **Pompidou Centre** in Paris decided that many of the building's famous exposed services were not required anymore. What should they put in their place?

Overdraw your ideas in the space provided...

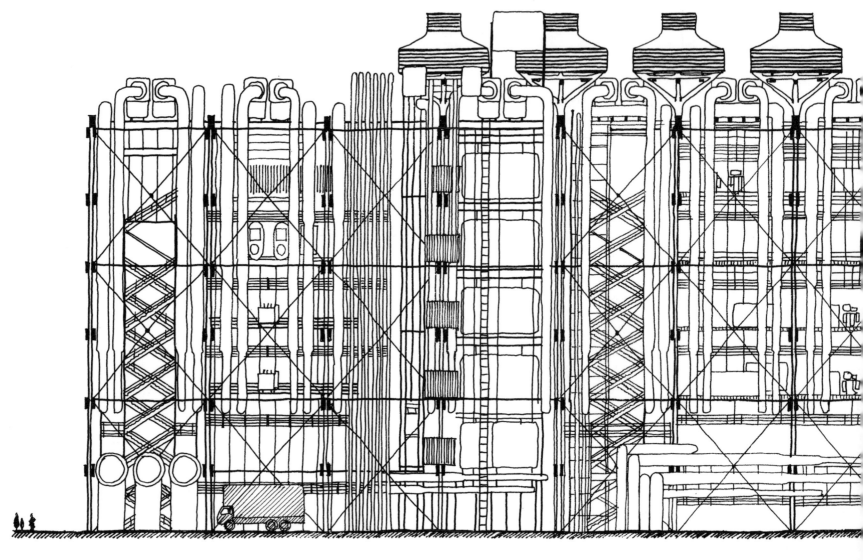

Pompidou Centre, Paris, France. Richard Rogers and Renzo Piano, 1977

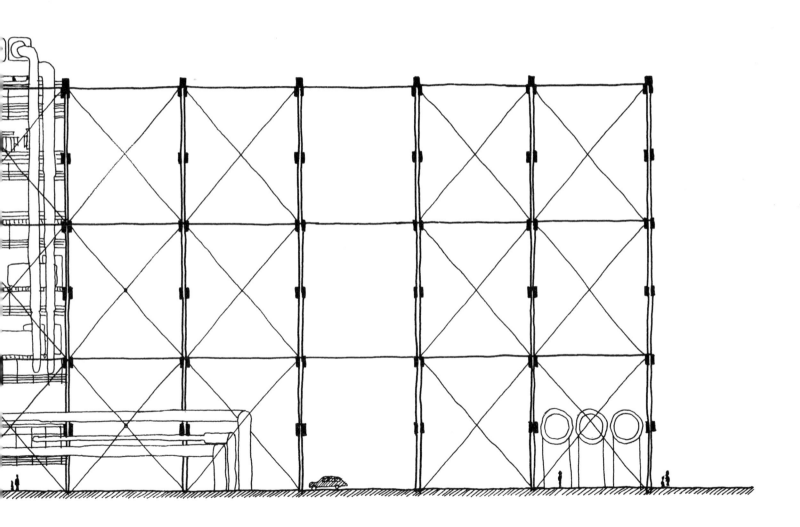

The form of many **modern museums** often express the
buildings' content. The two examples here express two very different ideas: one is a
work inspired by both sculpture and the surrounding former-shipyard area; the other
is a powerful expression of the Jewish people's historical struggle.

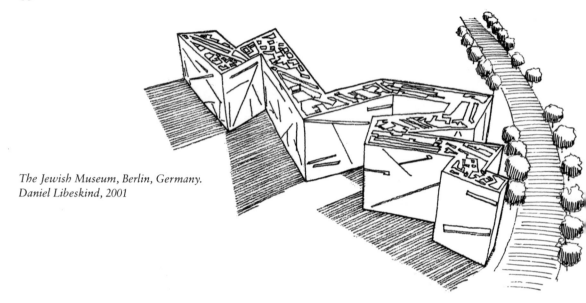

The Jewish Museum, Berlin, Germany.
Daniel Libeskind, 2001

The Guggenheim Museum, Bilbao, Spain.
Frank O. Gehry, 1997

Decide on a theme for a museum and sketch some architectural
forms that you feel best express the spirit of your proposal...

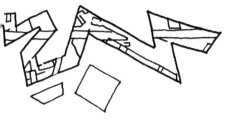

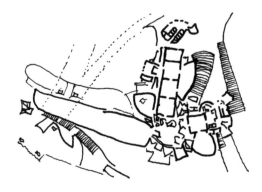

This mobile **Classroom of the Future** was designed by Gollifer Langston Architects in 2007. It can be transported by lorry from one location to another and provides workstations and audio/visual equipment.

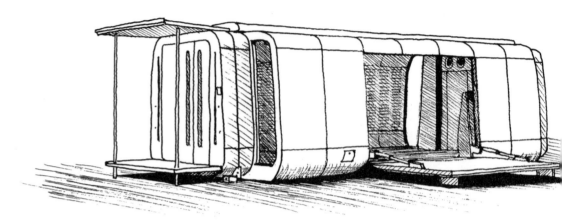

Design a mobile educational unit that would fit on a standard truck...

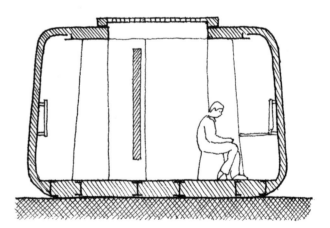

Classroom of the Future, London, England. Gollifer Langston Architects, 2007

Here is a selection of **designs for dogs** by different architects that will alter the way that the owners interact with their pets.

'Paramount' mirror for a poodle by Konstantin Grcic

'Pointed T' suspended cone to house a Japanese terrier by the Hara Design Institute

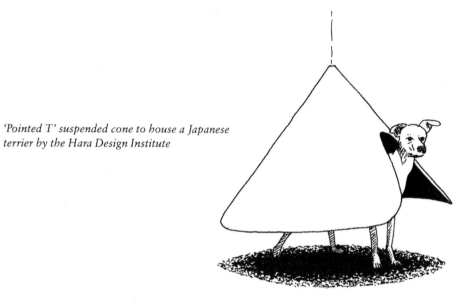

Draw some ideas for other domestic animals, such as this cat basket that hangs on a radiator...

Ramp for daschund by Atelier Bow-Wow

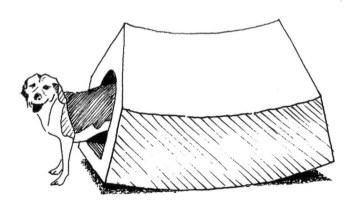

Rocking kennel for a beagle by MVRDV

This prototype **circular house** used mass-produced aircraft
technology and materials combined with an innovative rotating-roof ventilation system.

Design a house with a plan based on a circle...

Wichita House, Kansas, USA. Buckminster Fuller, 1947

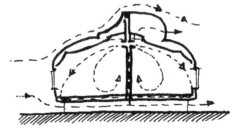

Diagram showing airflow due to roof ventilation system

Incorporating water into the design of an environment can have both a dramatic and a calming effect.

Sketch a place that you know, a garden or interior or even a public place, and design a new water feature within it...

*Private Residence, London, England.
Tankard Bowkett, 2007*

Church on the Water, Tomamu, Japan. Tadao Ando, 1988

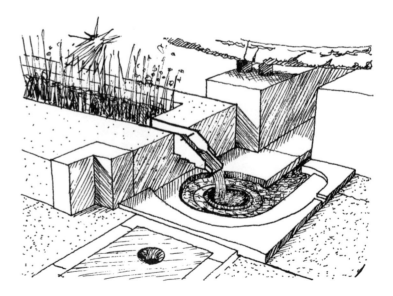

*Garden of the Fondazione Querini Stampalia, Venice, Italy.
Carlo Scarpa, 1963*

Fuente de los Amantes, Mexico.
Luis Barragán, 1966

Frank Lloyd Wright described his work as **'organic' architecture,** 'where the whole is (to) the part, what the part is to the whole.' His Fallingwater house completely integrated the surrounding landscape as part of the environment of the house.

Choose a particular location and, using 'organic' principles, sketch the design of a house that is integrated within its context...

Fallingwater, Pennsylvania, USA.
Frank Lloyd Wright, 1939

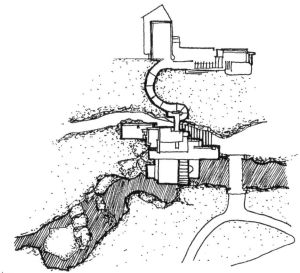

Aerial view

This is a **sectional drawing** of a hotel/spa that has been cut into the mountain over a thermal spring. The quartzite stone of the mountain is used to form the structure.

Using the same mountain slope, design in section the arrangement of a small thermal bath house. Consider views, light and privacy...

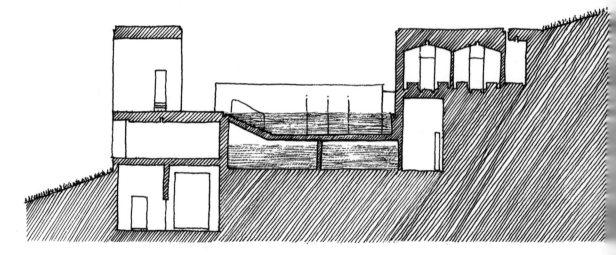

The Therme Vals, Switzerland.
Peter Zumthor, 1996

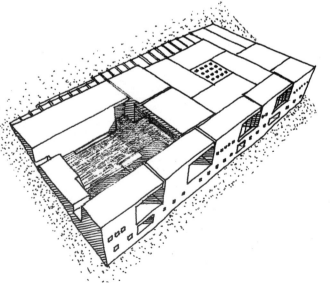

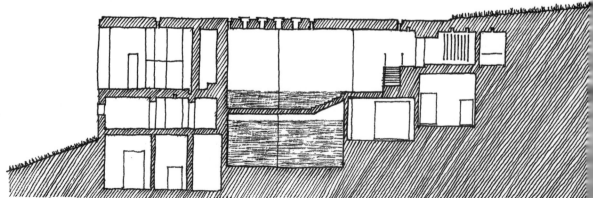

Breaking down **the threshold** between the street and gallery is the aim of this Storefront for Art and Architecture façade.

Sketch your proposal for a new design, with particular attention to the entrance...

The Storefront for Art and Architecture, New York, USA. Stephen Holl and Vito Acconci, 1993

Our major **cities of the future** are becoming taller, denser and a mixture of different styles and forms. This drawing of an imagined city is constructed using a variety of sampled projects and made-up forms and designs.

Complete the city panorama with your vision of the future.
Once completed give this city a name...

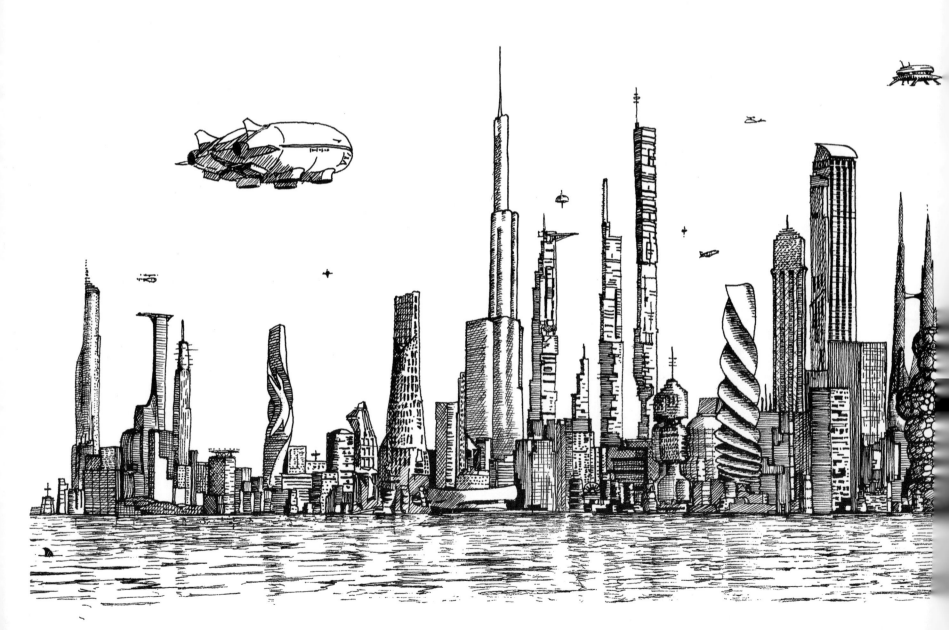

You've completed the book and won the award for **Architect of the Year!**

Design an award that you would be happy to receive...

Academy Award statuette ('Oscar'); The Pritzker Architecture Prize;
BAFTA Award; FIFA World Cup Trophy

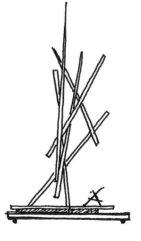

Credits & acknowledgements

All of the drawings in the book have been created by the author especially for this publication; some are based on the original drawings of architects and artists, and we are pleased to credit these below. In all cases, every effort has been made to credit the copyright holder, but should there be any omissions or errors the Publisher would be pleased to insert the appropriate acknowledgement in subsequent editions of this book.

The author would like to give many thanks to Jane Tankard for all of her encouragement, inspiration and time spent giving feedback. Also thanks to Philip Cooper, Gaynor Sermon and the team at Laurence King Publishing for their help, support and editorial dedication and to Matt Cox at Newman and Eastwood for designing the book.

Sketch of Falkestrasse rooftop renovation by Coop Himmelb(l)au, 1988
Typeface by Theo van Doesburg
Mae West Lips Sofa, Salvador Dalí, 1937 © Salvador Dalí, Fundació Gala-Salvador Dalí, DACS, 2013
Prototype Bauhaus font by Herbert Bayer, Dessau Bauhaus, 1925 © DACS 2013
Plan of The Chapel of Note Dame du Haut by Le Corbusier, 1954 © ADAGP, Paris and DACS, London 2013
'The Sixth Order or The End of Architecture' by Leon Krier
Comparative study of corner houses by Rob Krier
'Architectural Machines' by Yakov Chernikhov, 1931
Suprematist Composition by Kazimir Malevich, 1916
Lenin Tribune by El Lissitzsky, 1920
'I am a Monument' by Robert Venturi and Denise Scott Brown, 1972
Sketch of proposed National Stadium, Japan by Zaha Hadid, 2019
Plan of The Farnsworth House by Ludwig Mies van der Rohe, 1951 © DACS 2013
Plan of the Berlin Building Exhibition by Ludwig Mies van der Rohe and Lilly Reich, 1931 © DACS 2013.
Sketches of The Einstein Tower by Erich Mendelsohn, 1921
Plan of Gut Garkau Farm by Hugo Häring, 1926 © DACS 2013
Plan of The Storefront for Art and Architecture, New York, by Stephen Holl and Vito Acconci, 1993 © ARS, NY and DACS, London 2013 (Acconci only)